THE WTF CLAUSEBOOK

Vol - 1 For Contractors

A Satirical Survival Guide for Engineers in Construction

50 Clauses That Break Projects, Budgets, and Your Sanity

Fifty Clauses. Zero Common Sense.

JINOY VISWAN
(Definitely not a lawyer)

notionpress.com

INDIA • SINGAPORE • MALAYSIA

ISBN

Hardcase 979-8-90479-515-3
Paperback 979-8-90089-890-2

Disclaimer

This book is not legal advice. But let us be honest, if you are holding a contract and searching for a laugh, it is already too late.

The WTF Clausebook is a satirical survival guide. It exposes the baffling, the circular, the hypocritical, and the intellectually dishonest phrases that make up your average construction contract.

The clauses discussed in this book are drawn from real contracts, project experience, and repeated patterns observed across the industry. Some arise from direct execution experience, others from discussions with peers and practitioners, and many from disputes that have already played out in one form or another.

Every clause in here can be defended in court if you can afford to go there. What the lawyers will not tell you is:

- You probably will not survive the legal costs.
- You will lose six tenders fighting for one case.
- And your cashflow will be hit harder than your dignity.

Yes, this book pokes fun at clauses that can technically hold up. But it also reflects the harsh, undeniably stupid realities of small and medium contractors fighting Million-dollar contract claims with a 5-person office and a Gantt chart.

Most of the judgments are from English courts, not because they hold a monopoly on contractual madness, but because their decisions are public, reasoned, and written in a language I can cite without hiring a comparative law expert; had I strayed into other jurisdictions, I would have had to explain unfamiliar doctrines, translate obscure procedures, pretend to understand other legal systems, and admit, with minimal shame, that some of the citations were compiled with research assistance tools.

The cases in this book are used to illustrate how Common Law courts think about contract problems, not to explain the judgments in full. Many of these decisions deal with several legal issues well beyond the specific clause behaviour discussed here. The examples are drawn selectively from judgements to help engineers recognise how disputes are judged in practice, not to turn this book into a law textbook or a substitute for legal advice.

This book is written primarily through the lens of English common law, because its reasoning is explicit, precedent-driven, and widely adopted in international construction contracts.

The same clause can produce very different outcomes under different legal systems, even where facts appear identical.

But a word of advice to engineers and site teams: the governing law decides disputes only after everything else has failed.

The safest contract strategy is not to win in court, but to resolve issues on site, in writing, before the law ever gets the chance to intervene.

No part of this book should be construed as legal, financial, or existential advice. If you are unsure about a clause, a claim, or your will to live, consult a qualified lawyer (preferably one who will not bill you in six-minute increments for reading this disclaimer).

While this book is unapologetically satirical, the issues it highlights are real, recurring, and often catastrophic for those who do not read carefully or defend themselves early. Clauses have consequences, and poor drafting or blind acceptance of terms can, and frequently does, result in disputes, delays, cost overruns, and cashflow collapse. The commentary offered herein aims to encourage clearer understanding and more balanced application across all levels of the contracting chain.

Party Definitions

Let's get one thing straight before we get contractually confused. The following definitions are provided to avoid common misunderstandings that arise when real-world engineers, quantity surveyors, and project managers read terms assuming they mean what they say.

Employer

The party named in the Contract as the one with the money. May also be known as Client, Company, Owner, or The Entity That Approves Invoices Like It's a Constitutional Amendment. Responsible for issuing the scope, awarding the contract, and ghosting you for 45 business days. Capable of changing the schedule, the scope, and your blood pressure.

Engineer

The person or entity appointed by the Employer to act on its behalf in administering the Contract. Not necessarily an engineer by training, temperament, or toolbar. The Engineer frequently claims to be impartial, and just as frequently, copies the Employer on everything. Common duties include issuing Instructions, rejecting submittals, and pretending that the baseline programme was never approved.

Contractor

The party responsible for executing the works as per the Contract. That's you. Also known as Vendor, Builder, Execution Partner, or The One Who'll Be Blamed Anyway. Bound by deadlines, drawings, and decisions made three years ago in a boardroom with no windows. Enjoys the benefit of clear obligations and ambiguous entitlements.

Subcontractor

A party engaged by the Contractor to carry out part of the Works. Occasionally specialises in scope, but frequently in claims. Operates with a curious mixture of overconfidence and selective amnesia. Will always blame the Contractor's coordination, design, or "miscommunication on your side."

Consultant

A third-party expert who is appointed to advise the Employer on matters the Contractor has already explained six times. Paid handsomely to raise concerns and cite industry best practice. Never liable, rarely available, always copied.

Note: These definitions are satirical. But the damage caused by misunderstanding them? Very real.

Contents

To Daddy
1944 – 2026

Foreword

The first time I misunderstood a clause, it wasn't in a contract, it was in my marriage.
My wife said, "It's fine."
I thought it was fine.

It was **NOT**.

(Married people will understand. The unmarried should treat this as their first written early warning notice.)

That was my first brush with ambiguous language, delivered not by a lawyer, but by someone who knows how to say one thing and mean another with masterful precision. Later, when I began managing large EPC contracts, I realised something chilling:

Construction contracts are filled with "It's fine."

Clauses that look harmless until they explode. Sentences that promise clarity but deliver confusion. Phrases like "subject to mutual agreement at a later date" or "to the extent not inconsistent with the foregoing" that say everything and commit to nothing.

I have spent over three decades in the construction industry, on site, in boardrooms, across claims meetings, and bitter final accounts settlements. I have sat across tables from Employers who swore the clause meant one thing, and lawyers who swore it meant something else.

The truth?

It was just a bad clause. No one wanted to admit it. And eventually, I realised something deeper.

Understanding contract clauses is not optional. It is survival.

When I started writing this book, I struggled with the title. I wanted something powerful, something that reflected the frustration, confusion, and eye-rolling that every contract professional has experienced. I scribbled ideas, played with metaphors, and even flirted with legal Latin. Nothing landed. Zilch!

Then one day, I came across a particularly vague clause that said: "Unless otherwise inconsistent with the foregoing and subject to further mutual review and Employer understanding..."

And I blurted: "What the f*** is this?"

That was it. The Eureka moment. **WTF!**
I decided to call the book what most of us are actually thinking when we read those clauses. Yes, I know legal, and contract books are meant to be deep. But let us be honest, they often put you into deep sleep.
I wanted something different.

Something that you could read on a flight, mark up with a highlighter, pass to a colleague with a grin, and then quote in a client meeting when it really matters.

This book is not a textbook.

It is a survival guide.
A mirror.
A quiet smile in the middle of a very serious room.

Some clauses will make you chuckle.
Others will make you furious.
All of them are real.
And all of them are dangerous if misunderstood.

So read on. Learn, laugh, and never again sign a clause that makes you say: "Wait... what the f*** does that mean?"
Because in construction, every word has a cost code. And the most expensive ones are the ones you never questioned.

– Jinoy Viswan

This page left intentionally blank. Why... ? **WTF**.

About the Author

Jinoy Viswan is not a lawyer. He just reads contracts a bit better than others. And unlike most contract books, this one does not require caffeine, suffering, or legal Latin to survive.

Jinoy Viswan is an Engineer. With over 30 years in international EPC contracting, he has lived through every kind of clause-induced disaster: variations that were never instructed, delays that were always your fault, and notices that were too early, too late, or too polite to count.

He holds a Bachelor of Engineering, a Professional Diploma in Arbitration and also is pursuing his LLM in International Construction Contracts. He also vaguely remembers holding a whole bunch of other qualification acronyms and has absolutely no idea what half of them mean anymore. He is also Contracts-trained, delay-tested, and commercially battle-hardened.

This book is his survival guide. And his personal therapy.
And this book is not for Lawyers.
Especially not for Lawyers.

His passion? Helping engineers and project professionals stop signing contracts they do not understand and start defending the rights they already have.

This book is his way of arming them with wit, wisdom, and just enough legal awareness to keep the wolves at bay.
He wrote it for engineers, planners, project managers, and contract readers who stared at a clause and thought:

"Wait… what the f*** does that mean?"
Now you know you are not alone.
And finally, you have a book that tries to fight back.
The WTF Clausebook.
Happy reading.

How to Use this Book

This is not a textbook.
It will not help you pass a bar exam.
But it might stop you from signing something that could potentially bankrupt your contracting company, delay your payments, or costs you your Annual bonus.

This is a satirical survival guide for engineers who build real things, under contracts that quietly plan their demise.

You are not expected to read this book cover to cover in one sitting.
(Although I dare you to try. If you do, please send photos.)

Instead, think of it as:

- A first-aid kit for when the fine print gets too fine.
- A late-night companion during final account season
- Or just the book you throw across the room… before opening it again.
- Or, if nothing else works, the book you hit your client with, metaphorically. Probably. And hope ... WTF

This book is what happens when an engineer reads a contract, survives it, and decides to fight back, with sarcasm, case law, and red pens.

The legal principles referenced are predominantly drawn from common law jurisdictions and international arbitration practice. Local law outcomes may differ.

What You Will Find in Each Clause

Each clause is broken down into ten quick-hit sections:

Section	What It Tells You
Clause Title	As it often appears in real contracts
Satirical Subtitle	What it is secretly doing to your project
Engineer's Translation	The blunt reality
Satirical Interpretation	Why it is a setup
Why This Is a Problem	Where this clause hurts in practice
Legal Insight	Real case law, simplified
Where It Appears	Common clause placements
How to Fix It	Redlines, defences, and real-world edits
WTF Scoring System™	A scale of risk and absurdity
Engineering Takeaway	Your final punchline for the site meeting

Who This Book Is For

- Engineers who do not want to learn contract law, but must
- Project Managers who are tired of last-minute claim panic
- Quantity Surveyors and Planners who wish they had read the clause earlier.
- Contract Readers who want to fight back, without falling asleep

Whether you are preparing a claim, training your team, reviewing a tender, or just trying to avoid another unpleasant surprise, this book was written for you.

Pro Tips

- Use the WTF Scoring System™ to prioritise your clause reviews.
- Mark clauses you have seen in your own projects, you will find them.
- Use each entry as a training handout for your site teams.
- Quote it in your meetings. It is more fun than arguing with PowerPoint.

WTF Scoring System™

This book uses a highly unscientific, unreliable, completely irrational, not-at-all-legally-binding scoring system called the **WTF Scoring System™**.

Each clause is scored based on three metrics:

Metric	**What It Actually Means**
WTF Factor	How much this clause made us mutter "**What the f***?**" when we first read it. (A perfect ten means it was probably written on a Friday afternoon and never read again.)
Risk Profile	What level of chaos this clause will unleash. (High = LDs, Medium = headaches, Low = false sense of security.)
Verdict	What to do before this clause does something to you. (Delete, Rewrite, Cross-reference, or Pray.)

Scoring Scale:

Score Range	**Interpretation**
9.0–10.0	Lawyers wrote it. No one checked it. You are already in trouble.
8.0–8.9	It looks fine, until it destroys your claim in Week 47.
7.0–7.9	You will survive. But you will regret not redlining it.
6.0–6.9	Mildly annoying. Could be worse. Probably will be.
<6.0	This clause is suspiciously reasonable. Double-check for traps.

Welcome to The WTF Clausebook.
Because contracts may be written in ink,
but they are paid for in blood, time, and Liquidated Damages.

"If two words can contradict each other, a lawyer will most probably put them in the same sentence and call it clarity."

– Jinoy's Law on Contracts Drafting

"Consistency is the last refuge of the unimaginative." — Oscar Wilde

CLAUSE #01

"To the Extent not Otherwise Inconsistent with the Foregoing..."

aka: *The Clause That Eats Its Own Tail*

ENGINEER'S TRANSLATION:

"This clause applies, unless it clashes with something we said earlier. In which case, please figure it out."

Terminology Note: In this book, "Engineer"[1] refers to the role defined under the Contract (e.g., in The International Federation of Consulting Engineers, FIDIC Contracts), typically acting on behalf of the Employer.

"engineer" (lowercase) refers more broadly to any site/project/design engineer, often the poor weary soul caught between impossible clauses and immovable deadlines.

SATIRICAL INTERPRETATION:

This clause sounds like it was written by someone trying to cover all bases... and instead set the whole thing on fire.

---

1 The person or entity appointed by the Employer to act on its behalf in administering the Contract. See Party Definitions.

It walks into your contract with a confident tone, then immediately defers to the previous clause, just in case you misunderstood, or worse, understood it too well.

It is the legal version of saying:

"Everything I just said is valid unless I said something different earlier. Or later. Good luck."

WHY THIS IS A PROBLEM:

This clause is an interpretive time bomb. It introduces recursive logic into the contract, where clauses are qualified by others that are also being qualified. The result is a legal sentence that invalidates itself mid-way.

This clause is often bolted onto:

- Indemnities
- Limitation of liability
- Force majeure
- Risk allocation
- Scope disclaimers

But it creates internal inconsistency, because instead of resolving contradictions, it admits them.

Rather than state which clause takes precedence, it shrugs and says:

"Just follow whichever part makes more sense in the moment."

That is not contract drafting. That is verbal gymnastics with liability on the line.

LEGAL INSIGHT:

In *Chartbrook Ltd v Persimmon Homes Ltd*[2] [2009] UKHL 38, the House of Lords confirmed that contractual wording is interpreted by reference to

---

2 Chartbrook Ltd v Persimmon Homes Ltd [2009] UKHL 38, United Kingdom (House of Lords).

what a reasonable person, with the relevant background knowledge, would understand the parties to have meant. Where drafting has plainly gone wrong, courts may prefer a commercially sensible construction over a literal reading, but they will not rescue parties from uncertainty where the contract fails to state which provision prevails.

A phrase such as “to the extent not otherwise inconsistent with the foregoing” does not create order. It creates a priority question. If the contract does not identify which clause controls, the dispute shifts from performance to interpretation. That is where cost, time, and entitlement begin to bleed.

BUT IF IT IS MEANT TO PROTECT, WHY IS IT SO DANGEROUS?

Because instead of clarifying, it creates doubt about which clause governs.

Let us say Clause 12.3 limits the Contractor’s liability:
“The Contractor shall not be liable for any indirect, consequential, or special losses…”

Then Clause 12.4 follows with:
“To the extent not otherwise inconsistent with the foregoing, the Contractor shall indemnify the Employer…”
Now what happens if the Employer claims indirect losses?
Clause 12.3 says: No liability.
Clause 12.4 allows it, but only if it is consistent.

And you are back in court, arguing what the drafter should have written properly.

HOW TO FIX IT:

Delete this phrase unless there is a structural need to signal clause priority.

If one clause should prevail, say so clearly:

“This clause shall prevail in the event of conflict with Clause X.X.”

Or define precedence globally in the contract:

"In the event of conflict between provisions, the following order of precedence shall apply..."

Never leave priority open to interpretation, tribunals will interpret it for you.

WTF SCORING SYSTEM™

Metric	Score
WTF Factor	9.3/10 – Self-destructive modifier
Risk Profile	HIGH – Internal conflict risk
Verdict	DELETE or REPLACE with clear precedence language

ENGINEERING TAKEAWAY:

A contract is not a "Choose-Your-Own-Adventure." If your clause contradicts itself, or the one above it, you have already lost half the battle.

"If you can't dazzle them with brilliance, baffle them with nonsense."
– W.C. Fields

CLAUSE #02

"Without Prejudice to the Generality of the Foregoing..."

aka: *The Clause That Thinks You Weren't Listening*

ENGINEER'S TRANSLATION:

"I know I just said something. I am going to say it again. Differently. And hope it still makes sense."

SATIRICAL INTERPRETATION:

This clause is what happens when the drafter loses confidence halfway through the contract.

It tries to be helpful by saying:

"Just because we listed a few things above doesn't mean that's all there is."

But instead of clarifying scope, it often leaves you wondering:

"So... does this expand the clause above, override it, or contradict it?"

WHY THIS IS A PROBLEM:

This clause tries to sound clever but ends up confusing everyone. By clinging to the phrase "without prejudice to the generality of the foregoing," the drafter attempts to expand scope while preserving structure but ends up doing neither. What starts as a non-exhaustive list ends in open-ended interpretation, giving the other side license to argue for things never intended and turning an otherwise tight clause into a loophole generator.

This phrase appears most frequently in:

- Variation clauses
- Indemnities
- Scope statements
- Force majeure provisions
- Employer or Contractor obligations

It is intended to protect non-exhaustive lists, but when used carelessly, it:

- Adds ambiguity rather than removing it.
- Imitates legal precision while actually duplicating or diluting the original meaning.
- Opens the door for a party to argue broader interpretation than intended.

LEGAL INSIGHT:

In *Investors Compensation Scheme Ltd v West Bromwich Building Society*[3] [1998] 1 WLR 896, the House of Lords confirmed that contractual wording is interpreted through the eyes of a reasonable person with the relevant background knowledge, not by mechanical reliance on legal formulae. Commercial context matters, but it cannot turn vague drafting into certainty.

The phrase "without prejudice to the generality of the foregoing" may assist where a clause uses a non-exhaustive list. Used carelessly, however, it can blur whether the following words expand, qualify, or override the earlier

3 Investors Compensation Scheme Ltd v West Bromwich Building Society [1998] 1 WLR 896, United Kingdom (House of Lords).

wording. If ambiguity remains after normal interpretation, the wording may be construed against the party relying on it. The safer course is simple: say whether the list is exhaustive, illustrative, or subject to a defined precedence rule.

BUT ISN'T THIS CLAUSE MEANT TO PROTECT BROAD SCOPE?

Yes, but there is a better way to do that.

This phrase is typically used to prevent narrow reading of the clause before it. But by using such legalised filler, you introduce an unintentional hierarchy:

- Is the original clause "general"?
- Is this now the "specific" override?
- Which takes precedence?

The result?

Your scope clause becomes a loophole. Your indemnity becomes an invitation to stretch. Your delay claim defence becomes a debate on what "foregoing" includes.

HOW TO FIX IT:

Remove "without prejudice to the generality of the foregoing" unless:

- The previous clause includes a clearly limited list, AND
- You need to expand that list with open-ended language.

Better alternatives:

"Including, without limitation..."
"Such obligations shall include, but not be limited to..."

Use bullet points if you need to show a mix of examples and general principles. It is clearer, and courts respect clarity.

WTF SCORING SYSTEM™

Metric	Score
WTF Factor	8.7/10 – Legal padding at its worst
Risk Profile	MEDIUM – Scope creep & interpretation risk
Verdict	DELETE or REPLACE with non-ambiguous listing language

ENGINEERING TAKEAWAY:

If your clause needs to clarify itself with a second sentence,
the first sentence was not clear enough.
Draft better once. Not louder twice.

Construction Lessons Series 001

"In construction, common sense is a clause that never got approved."

"Never put off till tomorrow what you can avoid altogether." – Anonymous

CLAUSE #03

"Subject to Mutual Agreement at a Later Date…"

aka: *The Clause That Promised to Call You Back*

ENGINEER'S TRANSLATION:

"We have no idea yet. Let us fight about it later when it is more expensive."

SATIRICAL INTERPRETATION:

This clause is the legal equivalent of saying:

"Let's see how we feel when the pressure is on.

It pretends to be collaborative. It is the contractual equivalent of saying, 'Let's not fight now, let's schedule the argument for when it costs ten times more.

But in reality, it is a polite postponement of a guaranteed dispute.
It hides in contracts where people hope they will agree when it matters.
But spoiler: that is almost never how construction works. An "agreement to agree" lacks the certainty required for contract formation and is therefore unenforceable.

WHY THIS IS A PROBLEM:

This clause replaces contractual clarity with future hope. "Subject to mutual agreement at a later date" is a time bomb: unenforceable, undefined, and dangerously open-ended. It hands both parties a blank cheque for future disagreement, postponing difficult decisions until they become disputes, and making sure no one has any rights when the pressure hits.

You will often see this clause used in:

- Provisional sums
- Variation pricing
- Subcontractor onboarding
- Milestone definition
- Risk-sharing frameworks.

It looks harmless, but it builds in a contractual black hole. Why?

Because "mutual agreement later" is:

- Legally non-binding
- Commercially dangerous
- A delay magnet

This clause postpones scope finalisation, making cost, risk, and programme planning impossible to align or enforce. In design-build or EPC projects, this clause is often inserted to finalise utility corridor ownership, façade specification, or risk-sharing models, all of which become ticking time-bombs once the baseline is locked.

LEGAL INSIGHT:

In *Baird Textile Holdings Ltd v Marks & Spencer plc*[4] [2001] EWCA Civ 274, the Court of Appeal confirmed that long-standing commercial dealings and future expectations do not, by themselves, create a binding obligation where

4 Baird Textile Holdings Ltd v Marks & Spencer plc [2001] EWCA Civ 274, United Kingdom (Court of Appeal).

essential terms remain uncertain. An agreement to agree is not enforceable merely because both parties hoped the missing terms would be settled later.

In *RTS Flexible Systems Ltd*[5] *v Molkerei Alois Müller GmbH* [2010] UKSC 14, the Supreme Court confirmed that parties who begin performance before finalising all terms may still be bound if their words and conduct objectively show an intention to contract. But where material terms remain unresolved and no fallback mechanism exists, uncertainty remains fatal. A clause that postpones key commercial terms without a clear default route is not flexibility; it is a dispute waiting for pressure.

BUT WHAT IF PARTIES ACT ON GOOD FAITH?

That is exactly the problem. This clause is often dropped in because both sides "intend" to work it out later. But:

- What if the market price changes?
- What if the scope becomes contentious?
- What if one party gains commercial advantage by not agreeing?

Then the clause becomes a contractual void with no enforcement mechanism. And the project team is left stuck between goodwill and legal silence.

Even if the parties perform, the absence of a clear term means you cannot prove what was agreed, let alone what was breached.

HOW TO FIX IT:

Replace "subject to mutual agreement..." with clear obligation triggers, such as:

"The Parties shall finalise the [X] within 14 days of [event]."

"If no agreement is reached, the matter shall be referred to the Engineer/Dispute Board/arbitration."

5 RTS Flexible Systems Ltd v Molkerei Alois Müller GmbH [2010] UKSC 14, United Kingdom (Supreme Court).

"Until agreed otherwise, the default provisions in Clause X.X shall apply."

If flexibility is needed, define a fallback position, not an empty promise.

WTF SCORING SYSTEM™

Metric	Score
WTF Factor	8.8/10 – Legal padding at its worst
Risk Profile	MEDIUM – Scope creep & interpretation risk
Verdict	DELETE or REPLACE with non-ambiguous listing language

ENGINEERING TAKEAWAY:

"Mutual agreement later" is not collaboration.
It is a silence that grows more expensive over time.

A good contract defines what happens if you do **not** agree.

"The road to hell is paved with good intentions." – Proverb

CLAUSE #04

"The Contractor Shall Use Best/Reasonable/All Reasonable Endeavours..."

aka: *The Clause That Will Break You (If You Let It)*

ENGINEER'S TRANSLATION:

"Try. Try harder. Try until it hurts. Or until the dispute arises."

SATIRICAL INTERPRETATION:

This clause reads like a pep talk, but it is actually a performance obligation with teeth.

It says:

"Do your best. But if your best is not good enough, and you were not clear about what you were supposed to do, then prepare to be blamed."

What sounds like a motivational phrase often becomes a liability trap. It is the kind of encouragement that starts with a pat on the back and ends with a shove off the claims cliff.

WHY THIS IS A PROBLEM:

This clause pretends to be motivational but acts like a legal trap. Whether it says "best," "reasonable," or "all reasonable" endeavours, it imports a level of performance obligation without defining what that means. Courts treat each phrase differently, and unless the contract explains which standard applies and how far it goes, the Contractor ends up judged not on what they did, but on what they failed to imagine doing.

These phrases are used in clauses covering:

- Delay recovery and mitigation.
- Force majeure and disruption
- Variation execution
- Cooperation with the Employer
- Procurement or commissioning assistance
- Risk transfers in subcontract management.

The problem? They are rarely defined. And each phrase implies a different legal standard.

LEGAL INSIGHT:

Let us decode the difference.

Phrase	Legal Weight	Risk
Best endeavours	Highest – May require sacrificing your own commercial interest	High
All reasonable endeavours	Medium – May require exploring multiple reasonable options	Medium
Reasonable endeavours	Lowest – Try within reason; no duty to suffer or lose money	Low

In *RTI Ltd v MUR Shipping BV*[6] [2024] UKSC 18, the Supreme Court confirmed that a reasonable endeavours obligation does not require a party to accept non-contractual performance unless the contract clearly says so. Reasonable

6 RTI Ltd v MUR Shipping BV [2024] UKSC 18, United Kingdom (Supreme Court).

endeavours are measured against the contract, not against hindsight, pressure, or heroic sacrifice.

In *Jet2.com Ltd v Blackpool Airport Ltd*[7] [2012] EWCA Civ 417, the Court of Appeal confirmed that a best endeavours obligation can impose a real and commercially burdensome duty where that is necessary to achieve the contractual objective. The lesson is not that every contractor must sacrifice itself; it is that undefined endeavour wording allows someone else to argue how far your effort should have gone.

STILL CONFUSED? HERE IS HOW IT FEELS ON SITE:

- **Best endeavours**: *Trying your best in a contract like this is not about effort—it is about sacrifice. You're not just running a marathon with a piano on your back. You are tuning it mid-run, paying for transport, and expected to win the race too. That is what this clause is really demanding.*
- **All reasonable endeavours**: *Run hard. Explore all possible routes. Carry your own spares.*
- **Reasonable endeavours**: *Jog if it makes sense. Walk if it saves money. Stop if it ruins your float.*

In *Jet2.com Ltd v Blackpool Airport Ltd*, the Court of Appeal held that a party under a "best endeavors" obligation cannot be avoided because it became commercially inconvenient. Even when the underlying agreement did not mandate commercial loss, the best endeavors clause created a duty to pursue outcomes actively, unless performance becomes genuinely impossible. This judgment reinforced that "best" means real effort, not just intent.

THE REAL DANGER?

Because these terms are undefined, disputes often turn into retrospective judgment calls:

"Did you do enough?"
"Was there another reasonable thing you could have done?"
"Did you stop short of your 'best'?"

---

7 Jet2.com Ltd v Blackpool Airport Ltd [2012] EWCA Civ 417, United Kingdom (Court of Appeal).

If you cannot prove your effort aligned with the clause level, you may be seen as non-compliant, even if the outcome was not your fault.

HOW TO FIX IT:

Define the level of effort expected. Do not leave it to tribunal interpretation.

"Reasonable endeavours shall not require the Contractor to incur material cost, redeploy critical resources, or interrupt obligations to third parties."

Match the level of endeavour to the risk level:

- Use reasonable for general cooperation.
- Use all reasonable if multiple options exist, but time/money matter.
- Avoid best unless you are truly ready to sacrifice your interest.

Never stack the terms (e.g., "best and all reasonable endeavours"), courts hate it, and it adds nothing but confusion.

WTF SCORING SYSTEM™

Metric	Score
WTF Factor	8.9/10 – Sounds soft, strikes hard
Risk Profile	HIGH – Performance obligation with undefined limits
Verdict	DEFINE or REPLACE with tangible performance metrics

ENGINEERING TAKEAWAY:

In contracts, "try" is not a suggestion.
It is a standard of performance.

If you do not define what that standard is, someone else will, when it is too late.

"A project schedule is reinforced optimism—strong on paper, cracks under load."

– Jinoy's Law on Time for Completion

"Punctuality is the thief of time." – Oscar Wilde

CLAUSE #05

"Time is of the Essence... Unless Otherwise Agreed By the Parties."

aka: *The Clause That Gave Up Halfway*

ENGINEER'S TRANSLATION:

"Time really, really matters, until it does not. We will let you know. Maybe."

SATIRICAL INTERPRETATION:

This clause reads like a foreman yelling 'We're already late!' before taking a two-week coffee break. It starts strong and serious, but before you can react, it's already softened into an excuse,

"...unless we both agree to ignore it later."

It wants to sound forceful but builds in its own undoing.

WHY THIS IS A PROBLEM:

This clause tries to declare urgency while building in its own undoing. "Time is of the essence... unless otherwise agreed" sounds assertive, but in practice it creates doubt. It invites silence to be misread as flexibility, delays to be excused informally, and enforcement to collapse later under the weight of contradictory conduct. It turns a schedule safeguard into a waiver minefield.

This clause is often used to:

- Justify Liquidated Damages
- Trigger termination after delay.
- Emphasise milestone deadlines.
- Anchor an "essential obligation."

But by adding "unless otherwise agreed," it:

- Implies flexibility without process.
- Suggests that time is waivable by silence.
- Risks waiver by conduct if the Employer delays but does not enforce.

Time becomes 'of the essence' where:

a. it is expressly stated;
b. the nature of the contract demands it (e.g. perishable goods); or
c. one party makes it so via clear notice after delay.

In construction, clauses that say 'time is not of the essence' are often inserted by Employers to avoid having their own delays treated as material breach, while still enforcing LDs against Contractors. Courts scrutinise such asymmetries

LEGAL INSIGHT:

In *United Scientific Holdings Ltd v Burnley Borough Council*[8] [1978] AC 904, the House of Lords confirmed that time is not automatically "of the essence" unless the contract, the surrounding circumstances, or a valid notice makes it so. A party that declares time to be critical must then act consistently with that position, or risk creating waiver, uncertainty, or dispute over enforcement.

In *Behzadi v Shaftesbury Hotels Ltd*[9] [1992] Ch 1, the Court of Appeal confirmed that, after default, time may be made of the essence by notice, but the notice must allow a reasonable time for performance. The lesson is simple: if time is essential, the contract must say so clearly, the parties must behave consistently, and any later flexibility must be recorded in writing.

---

8 United Scientific Holdings Ltd v Burnley Borough Council [1978] AC 904, United Kingdom (House of Lords).

9 Behzadi v Shaftesbury Hotels Ltd [1992] Ch 1, United Kingdom (Court of Appeal).

BUT WAIT, IF TIME IS OF THE ESSENCE, WHY HAVE EOT CLAUSES?

Great question. This clause often appears alongside a full Extension of Time mechanism, which seems contradictory.

But it is not. Here is why:

"Time is of the essence" = Legal trigger

It means a failure to meet the deadline is a material breach, allowing termination or damages.

EOT clauses = Commercial flexibility

They allow the completion date to be adjusted lawfully for excusable events (e.g., variations, force majeure, employer delays) without triggering default.

Together, they preserve balance:

- EOT protects the contractor from wrongful LDs.
- "Time is of the essence" protects the employer from endless extensions.

In fact, if no EOT clause existed and the employer caused delay, the contract could fall into "Time at Large," where LDs become unenforceable and the contractor need only complete in a "reasonable time".

So yes, both clauses can and should exist, but only if they are clearly drafted and properly enforced.

HOW TO FIX IT:

Be explicit and binary. Either:

"Time is of the essence for all obligations in Clause X.X, and this shall not be waived unless expressly agreed in writing."

Or if flexibility is needed:

"Time is not of the essence. Delays may entitle the other party to remedies subject to Clause X.X."

Avoid vague hybrids. They confuse the contract, the contractor, and eventually, the Courts.

WTF SCORING SYSTEM™

Metric	Score
WTF Factor	8.8/10 – Starts strong, ends vague
Risk Profile	HIGH – Waiver by conduct risk
Verdict	REWRITE TO BE BINARY AND CLEAR

ENGINEERING TAKEAWAY:

If time is not of the essence, then deadlines are polite requests… until they become Exhibit A in a termination letter.

If time is of the essence, act like it.
Enforce every deadline. Issue every notice.

Because if you delay… the clause may not save you.

Construction Lessons Series 002

"Nothing moves a project faster than a deadline that already passed."

"Verbal contracts aren't worth the paper they're written on." – Samuel Goldwyn

CLAUSE #06

"Unless Otherwise Instructed in Writing, Which May Be Oral or Implied..."

aka: *The Clause That Forgot What 'Writing' Means*

ENGINEER'S TRANSLATION:

"Do not do anything unless told in writing.

Except if someone maybe said something that maybe implied it. Probably on site.

Possibly over lunch."

SATIRICAL INTERPRETATION:

This clause is what happens when legal drafting self-destructs in the same sentence.

It starts with certainty:
"Only written instructions are valid."

Then immediately undermines itself by saying:
"...which may be oral or implied."
So is it writing? Or is it a look, a nod, and a Teams chat?

It is like saying:
"This must be a formal email. Or a whisper. Or maybe a feeling."

WHY THIS IS A PROBLEM:

This clause commits the ultimate self-own. It demands written instructions, then immediately allows them to be oral or implied. The result is a contract that enforces nothing, validates everything, and undermines the very rule it sets. It does not just confuse the parties, it sets them up to fight about whether a conversation was an instruction, and whether a gesture was a binding variation.

You will find this clause lurking in:

- Variation and change instruction clauses.
- Site directions and approvals
- Temporary works and design interfaces
- Force majeure adjustments

It attempts to give flexibility in fast-moving environments. But it does so by breaking the contract's own rules of evidence.

The result?

- Verbal instructions become binding, without paper trail.
- Implied consent becomes actual liability.
- Site engineers get ambushed by *"But I told your supervisor!"*

If your contract says instructions must be written, but also says oral or implied instructions apply, you have created a paradox. And courts hate paradoxes.

LEGAL INSIGHT:

If a contract requires instructions or variations to be in writing, courts will usually give serious weight to that formality. In *Rock Advertising Ltd v MWB*[10] *Business Exchange Centres Ltd* [2018] UKSC 24, the Supreme Court confirmed

10 Rock Advertising Ltd v MWB Business Exchange Centres Ltd [2018] UKSC 24

that clauses requiring written variation will generally be upheld, and that oral agreement or informal conduct alone will not usually override a clear "no oral modification" clause.

In *RTS Flexible Systems Ltd v Molkerei Alois Müller GmbH*[11] [2010] UKSC 14, the Supreme Court also confirmed that parties may still become bound by their conduct where their words and actions objectively show an intention to proceed on agreed terms. That is the danger in mixed drafting: one sentence demands writing, while the next invites oral or implied instruction. The result is uncertainty over authority, hierarchy, proof, and entitlement.

BUT ISN'T FLEXIBILITY IMPORTANT ON SITE?

Yes, but not at the expense of clarity.

Site instructions need speed. But that does not mean we allow:

- Unrecorded commitments
- Informal variations
- Contractor obligations triggered by suggestion, hint, or site politics.

This clause, as drafted, gives maximum exposure and minimum enforceability.

The Employer can say:
"We told you."

You can say:
"Where's the instruction?"

And the clause says:
"Good luck resolving this."

11 RTS Flexible Systems Ltd v Molkerei Alois Müller GmbH [2010] UKSC 14

HOW TO FIX IT:

Separate the forms of instruction. For example:

"The Contractor shall act only on written instructions issued by the Engineer. Oral directions may be followed only if confirmed in writing within two working days."

Add escalation protocol:

"Unconfirmed instructions shall not bind either party unless formally recorded and approved."

Avoid layering contradictory language. If writing is required, then **mean it.**

WTF SCORING SYSTEM™

Metric	Score
WTF Factor	9.2/10 – One clause, three interpretations
Risk Profile	HIGH – Instructional chaos & liability exposure
Verdict	RESTRUCTURE or CLARIFY hierarchy & format

ENGINEERING TAKEAWAY:

If everything is "written"... and also "oral"... and also "implied," then nothing is reliable. And in construction, reliability is how you get paid.

Write it clear or lose it all.

Construction Lessons Series 003

"The more perfect the specification, the less chance it has of surviving reality."

"The more I explain it, the less you understand." – Mark Twain

CLAUSE #07

"For the Avoidance of Doubt..."

***aka:** The Clause That Introduced Even More Doubt*

ENGINEER'S TRANSLATION:

"Let me clarify something you were not confused about… until now."

SATIRICAL INTERPRETATION:

This clause wants to sound helpful.
Reassuring. Clean.
But it is actually whispering:
"I am about to say something that slightly contradicts what we just said above. But not really. Or maybe..."

It is like someone saying:

"Just to be clear, this does not change anything." And you immediately think: *"Wait... change what?"*

WHY THIS IS A PROBLEM:

This clause pretends to clarify but actually raises new doubts. "For the avoidance of doubt..." is often followed by a contradiction, a rephrasing, or a list that subtly rewrites the base clause. Instead of resolving ambiguity, it introduces reassurance into revision, and clarity into confusion disguised as legal neatness.

You will often find this phrase used to:

- Reframe indemnity clauses.
- Carve out exclusions in liability.
- Emphasise something already said.
- Add lists under general obligations.

It is a phrase that tries to clarify scope but often distorts the original intention.

It gives a false sense of security. In many cases, it reintroduces ambiguity, by trying to hedge or expand what is already covered.

LEGAL INSIGHT:

The phrase "for the avoidance of doubt" can assist where it genuinely clarifies an existing obligation. But courts will not treat it as magic wording. In *Investors Compensation Scheme Ltd*[12] *v West Bromwich Building Society* [1998] 1 WLR 896, the House of Lords confirmed that contractual meaning is assessed by reference to context and commercial sense, not by isolated legal formulae.

In *Chartbrook Ltd v Persimmon Homes Ltd*[13] [2009] UKHL 38, the House of Lords confirmed that where language has plainly gone wrong, courts may prefer the meaning a reasonable person would understand the parties to have intended. If a so-called clarification contradicts or materially changes the main clause, it may be treated as a qualification, an override, or an ambiguity, not a clarification.

---

12 Investors Compensation Scheme Ltd v West Bromwich Building Society [1998] 1 WLR 896, United Kingdom (House of Lords).

13 Chartbrook Ltd v Persimmon Homes Ltd [2009] UKHL 38, United Kingdom (House of Lords).

SO WHY DO DRAFTERS KEEP USING IT?

Because it feels safer to repeat things.
Because it sounds precise.
Because some lawyers believe that saying something twice makes it stronger.

But the reality is:

- If the original clause was clear, this adds nothing.
- If the original clause was vague, this makes it worse.
- If used in a list, it implies exclusivity or override that might not be intended.

That is not clarification. That is contract word spaghetti.

HOW TO FIX IT:

First, ask: Is this clause even necessary? If the base clause is clear, remove the clarification.

If you must use it, follow it with precision, not repetition.

Replace with:

"This clause includes, but is not limited to, the following..."
"The intent of this clause is to clarify that [specific outcome] applies."

Avoid using it as a verbal crutch.

WTF SCORING SYSTEM™

Metric	Score
WTF Factor	8.5/10 – Fake clarity alert
Risk Profile	MEDIUM – Creates silent contradictions
Verdict	Use only with targeted clarity or delete entirely

ENGINEERING TAKEAWAY:

If your clarification introduces confusion, then you did not avoid doubt.

You rebranded it.

"Common sense is not so common." – Voltaire

CLAUSE #08

"As May Be Reasonably Required By the Employer..."

aka: *The Clause That Opens the Door (But Hides the Key)*

ENGINEER'S TRANSLATION:

"We will let you know what we want. When we want. Based on what we think is reasonable. Good luck planning."

SATIRICAL INTERPRETATION:

This clause walks into your contract like a polite guest:

"Only what's reasonable, promise."

But what it does next depends entirely on the mood of the Employer.

What is "reasonable"?

- A new submission?
- Extra documentation?
- A full rework at your cost?

You are not told. You are told they will decide later.

WHY THIS IS A PROBLEM:

This clause opens the door for Employer discretion, without defining where it ends. "As may be reasonably required" sounds polite and flexible, but in reality, it operates like a wildcard: enabling scope creep, shifting obligations, and triggering silent variations without formal change. What is "reasonable" becomes whatever the Employer decides it is, after the fact.

You will find this phrase tucked into:

- Submittals and documentation clauses
- Scope alignment language
- Variation preambles
- EPC Employer's support obligations
- Contractor deliverable appendices

The danger is not in the word "required," it is in the word "reasonable," left entirely undefined.

This clause gives the Employer:

- Discretion without bounds
- Control without accountability.
- And scope expansion without compensation

It often becomes a silent variation clause that avoids the word "variation."

LEGAL INSIGHT:

In *Abbey Developments Ltd v PP Brickwork Ltd*[14] [2003] EWHC 1987 (TCC), the court treated a contractual power affecting scope as bounded by the contract itself, not as a licence to rewrite the bargain. A power to require, omit, or adjust work must still operate within the contractual framework.

In *Mid Essex Hospital Services NHS Trust v Compass Group UK and Ireland Ltd*[15] [2013] EWCA Civ 200, the Court of Appeal confirmed that contractual

14 Abbey Developments Ltd v PP Brickwork Ltd [2003] EWHC 1987 (TCC), United Kingdom (Technology and Construction Court).

15 Compass Group UK and Ireland Ltd v Mid Essex Hospital Services NHS Trust [2013] EWCA Civ 200, United Kingdom (Court of Appeal).

discretion must not be exercised arbitrarily, capriciously, or irrationally, and must be used for the purpose for which it was conferred. Applied here, "as may be reasonably required" is not a blank cheque. It must be tied to scope, deliverables, procedure, and the variation mechanism.

WHY THIS BECOMES A CLAIMS NIGHTMARE

Let us say the Employer issues a late instruction and says:

"It was reasonably required. You should have planned for it."

Your variation claim is now at risk of being dismissed because:

- The instruction was framed as "clarification."
- The base clause said, "as reasonably required."
- The Employer interprets that as entitlement-neutral.

Now you are fighting for:

- Time
- Money
- Recognition that something actually changed.

But the contract says they were simply exercising a clause.

HOW TO FIX IT:

Add boundaries to "reasonably required." For example:

"Requirements issued by the Employer shall be in writing, subject to Clause X.X [Variations], and shall not alter scope, timing, or cost without formal Agreement."

Or:

"Nothing in this clause shall obligate the Contractor to perform additional work outside the agreed Scope unless instructed in accordance with Clause X.X."

Be wary of "soft trigger" clauses, where something that sounds small causes project-wide consequences.

WTF SCORING SYSTEM™

Metric	Score
WTF Factor	8.8/10 – The Hidden Scope Trigger
Risk Profile	HIGH – Discretion without compensation
Verdict	REDEFINE or LINK to variation clause

ENGINEERING TAKEAWAY:

If the Employer can change your obligations by what they "reasonably require," then the scope is fluid, the contract is diluted, and your risk is unlimited.

You no longer have a contract. You have a wish list with consequences.

Demand clear limits, or it's just a wish with a price tag.

"Every law applies—especially the ones no one has heard of."

– Jinoy's Law on Compliance Law

Construction Lessons Series 004

"Contracts are written by optimists and enforced by opportunists."

"Ignorance of the law excuses no man—yet no man knows the law." – Proverb

CLAUSE #09

"The Contractor Shall Comply with all Applicable Laws, Regulations Known or Unknown..."

aka: *The Clause That Was Drafted by a Psychic*

ENGINEER'S TRANSLATION:

"You are responsible for obeying every law.
Even the ones that do not exist yet.
Even the ones no one told you about.
Even the ones no one has written."

SATIRICAL INTERPRETATION:

This clause is a masterstroke of risk transfer.

It begins reasonably:

"Comply with all applicable laws." Then it silently expands to include:
"...even if they change tomorrow, next year, or after the contract ends."

It turns you into a fortune teller, with no commercial fallback.

WHY THIS IS A PROBLEM:

This clause looks like a basic compliance line, until you realize it applies to laws that do not exist yet. "Known or unknown" turns a simple legal obligation into a forward-facing liability trap. You are now responsible not just for current legislation, but also for future regulatory shifts, without pricing, without warning, and without recourse.

You will find this clause in every EPC, FIDIC, and bespoke contract. The danger lies in its silence on time:

- Does "applicable laws" mean laws at the time of signing?
- Or laws at the time of performance?
- Or future laws that no one could have anticipated?

In long-term contracts, especially across multiple jurisdictions, this becomes a floating obligation:

- It changes scope.
- It increases cost.
- It opens liability without compensation.

LEGAL INSIGHT:

In *National Carriers Ltd v Panalpina (Northern) Ltd*[16] [1981] AC 675, the House of Lords confirmed that a supervening event will rarely discharge contractual obligations unless it makes performance impossible or radically different from what was agreed. Increased difficulty, delay, or cost is usually not enough.

Applied to this clause, the danger is clear. If the contract does not define whether "applicable laws" means laws at tender, award, execution, or future performance, the Contractor may inherit compliance risk that was never priced. Without a change-in-law mechanism, future regulation becomes a contractor's cost problem rather than a contractual relief event.

---

16 National Carriers Ltd v Panalpina (Northern) Ltd [1981] AC 675, United Kingdom (House of Lords).

WHERE THIS HURTS THE CONTRACTOR

This clause typically triggers claims and exposure in:

- Environmental law updates
- Labour law reforms
- Tax law or import/export controls
- Health & safety standards
- Force majeure reinterpretations

You quote based on today's law. But you may be forced to perform under tomorrow's regime, at your own cost.

HOW TO FIX IT:

Define the timeframe:

"...shall comply with all laws in force at the time of Contract signature and any subsequently enacted legislation that directly affects the Works, subject to Clause X.X [Variations or Change in Law]."

Insert a relief mechanism:

"If compliance with any new legislation materially affects time, cost, or method, the Contractor shall be entitled to relief in accordance with Clause X.X."

Never assume that "applicable laws" means "reasonable laws."

It simply means **all of them**, including the ones **not yet born.**

WTF SCORING SYSTEM™

Metric	Score
WTF Factor	9.0/10 – Psychic drafting meets passive risk transfer
Risk Profile	HIGH – Future legislation, undefined impact
Verdict	DEFINE applicability window or LINK to relief clause

ENGINEERING TAKEAWAY:

'Applicable laws' seems okay, but adds laws you can't know or price! A contract should share risks, not make you a crystal ball.

Set clear law rules now!

"Power tends to corrupt, and absolute power corrupts absolutely." – Lord Acton

CLAUSE #10

"Notwithstanding Anything to the Contrary Contained Herein…"

aka: *The Clause That Thinks It's the Boss of the Contract*

ENGINEER'S TRANSLATION:

"Ignore everything else we said, because this clause said so."

SATIRICAL INTERPRETATION:

This clause enters the contract like a bulldozer with a briefcase.

It looks around and says:

"You may have thought Clause 14.6 was clear. You may have relied on Clause 9.2. You may have signed off on Clause 7.4. But I am here now."

It does not just create exceptions.
It creates conflict.

WHY THIS IS A PROBLEM:

This clause thinks it outranks the entire contract. By starting with "Notwithstanding anything to the contrary…", it elevates itself above all other provisions, even when it should not. Without a clause hierarchy or clear scope, it invites interpretive chaos, overriding entitlements, nullifying safeguards, and turning the contract into a legal tug-of-war where this clause pulls hardest.

This phrase is:

- Overused
- Understood by few.
- Feared by many.

It appears in:

- Priority payment clauses
- Indemnity and exclusion provisions
- Termination rights
- Confidentiality overrides
- Force majeure carve-outs.

Its purpose is to elevate the clause it is in above all others. But unless the contract includes a clear hierarchy of clauses or documents, this phrase becomes anarchy in a sentence.

LEGAL INSIGHT:

"Notwithstanding" language can be effective, but courts will look closely at what it is overriding and whether the intention is expressed clearly. A clause cannot safely be treated as superior merely because it opens with powerful words; its scope, subject matter, and relationship with the rest of the contract must still be identified.

In *Macdonald Estates plc v Regenesis (2005) Dunfermline Ltd*[17] [2007] CSOH 123, the court recognised that "notwithstanding" wording may operate where the clause is clear in context. In *Australian Broadcasting Corp v XIVth Commonwealth Games Ltd*[18] [1988] 18 NSWLR 540, the court similarly treated

---

17 Macdonald Estates plc v Regenesis (2005) Dunfermline Ltd [2007] CSOH 123, Scotland (Outer House, Court of Session).

18 Australian Broadcasting Corporation v XIVth Commonwealth Games Ltd (1988) 18 NSWLR 540, Australia (New South Wales Court of Appeal).

override wording as dependent on clear intention. The lesson is simple: position matters, scope matters, and clarity matters most.

WHY THIS CLAUSE CAN BREAK YOUR ENTITLEMENT

Let us say:

- Clause 11.1 gives you the right to claim a delay cost.
- Clause 18.2 (later) starts with "Notwithstanding anything to the contrary..."

If 18.2 limits compensation to force majeure only, guess what?

Your claim under Clause 11.1 is gone. Because this one clause said it is in charge.

This clause can:

- Override entitlement
- Cancel exclusions.
- Undermine variations, indemnities, even EOT mechanisms.

HOW TO FIX IT:

If used, position it strategically and sparingly, not as a default prefix.

Always accompany it with:

"This clause shall apply notwithstanding any conflicting provisions of Clause X.X and Clause Y.Y."

Better yet, build a Clause Hierarchy Table in your contract:

"In the event of inconsistency, the following order of precedence shall apply..."

Never use this clause to patch up poor drafting. Fix the contradiction at its source.

"Include references to exactly which clauses it overrides and explain its necessity to avoid unintended waivers of other entitlements."

WTF SCORING SYSTEM™

Metric	Score
WTF Factor	9.2/10 – The Self-Appointed King Clause
Risk Profile	HIGH – Overrides structure, causes interpretive wars
Verdict	LIMIT, POSITION with care, or HIERARCHISE expressly

ENGINEERING TAKEAWAY:

If a clause can cancel others without warning, you do not have a contract.

You have a power struggle in paragraphs.

Construction Lessons Series 005

"Every change order proves that the original design was a theory in need of a scapegoat."

You can satisfy some of the people all of the time, you can satisfy all of the people some of the time, but you can't satisfy all of the people all of the time – John Lydgate

CLAUSE #11

"To the Satisfaction of the Engineer/Employer..."

aka: *The Clause That Turns Everyone into a Mind Reader*

ENGINEER'S TRANSLATION:

You must do the work. But it only counts if we say we like it.

SATIRICAL INTERPRETATION:

This clause gives your performance a new benchmark:

Not quality.
Not compliance.
Not spec.
Just... **satisfaction.**

But whose satisfaction?
The Engineer who visited once this month?
The Employer who reads drawings like a tea leaf?
You are left working to a moving target with no calibration. It is like saying:

"Run the race. We will decide the finish line later."

WHY THIS IS A PROBLEM:

This clause replaces objective standards with personal taste. It elevates "satisfaction" from a mood into a legal metric, allowing Engineers or Employers to override compliance with nothing more than a feeling. The risk? You meet the spec, pass the test... and still fail the clause, because someone, somewhere, is not "satisfied" This clause appears in:

- Inspection and test approvals
- Method statement acceptance
- Handover protocols
- Completion and milestone certifications
- Variation close-outs

It sounds harmless, after all, "satisfaction" implies acceptance.

But in law, it introduces:

- **Subjectivity** into performance criteria
- **Unilateral discretion** over certification
- A **breach risk** even after you have technically complied.

If your clause does not define what "satisfaction" is, you will be chasing smoke.

LEGAL INSIGHT:

Satisfaction clauses are not automatically invalid, but they are dangerous when they replace measurable standards with personal judgment. Where a contract gives one party an evaluative discretion, that discretion should be exercised honestly, rationally, and for the purpose for which it was conferred.

In *Mid Essex Hospital Services NHS Trust v Compass Group UK and Ireland Ltd*[19] [2013] EWCA Civ 200, the Court of Appeal drew an important distinction between a true contractual discretion and the exercise of an absolute contractual right. Applied here, "satisfaction" should not become an unlimited veto. If

19 Mid Essex Hospital Services NHS Trust v Compass Group UK and Ireland Ltd [2013] EWCA Civ 200, United Kingdom (Court of Appeal).

the clause does not define objective criteria, the Contractor is left proving irrationality after the damage has already been done.

WHERE THIS TURNS AGAINST YOU

Let us say:

- You submit test results that meet every spec.
- But the Engineer writes: "Not satisfactory. Retest."
- Or the Employer says: "We are not satisfied with the finish."

There is no appeal. No metric. No process.

You are back to square one, with time lost and cost unrecoverable.

HOW TO FIX IT:

- Clarify whose satisfaction governs the clause.
- Define the basis of satisfaction:

"To the satisfaction of the Engineer, acting reasonably and in accordance with the Contract Specifications."

- Add backup wording:

"Satisfaction shall not be unreasonably withheld where the Works conform to contractual requirements."

- Where possible, **replace "satisfaction" with objective standards**:
    - Tolerances
    - Measurable tests
    - Approvals by reference to documented criteria

WTF SCORING SYSTEM™

Metric	Score
WTF Factor	8.6/10 – Compliance Without Closure
Risk Profile	HIGH – Opens entitlement to discretionary override
Verdict	REPLACE with objective criteria or limit discretion

ENGINEERING TAKEAWAY:

You can pass a test or meet a rule, but 'satisfaction' is just their opinion with control! Use clear tests, not feelings.

"A 'no' uttered from deepest conviction is better than a 'yes' merely to please."
– Mahatma Gandhi

CLAUSE #12

"Shall not Unreasonably Withhold Consent..."

aka: *The Clause That Never Says Yes, But Will Never Admit It*

ENGINEER'S TRANSLATION:

"You need permission.
They might not give it.
But if they do not, they will say it was reasonable."

SATIRICAL INTERPRETATION:

This clause pretends to be helpful.
It says:

"We will not unreasonably say no."

But it never says what counts as "unreasonable." So it becomes the polite way to deny things forever.

And the beauty of it?
You have to prove that their silence or refusal was unreasonable.
Which is... beautifully impossible.

WHY THIS IS A PROBLEM:

This clause creates the illusion of fairness. "Shall not unreasonably withhold consent" sounds cooperative, but it grants veto power without clear rules and shifts the burden of proof onto you. The result? A silent "No", a delayed "maybe", or a never-ending wait, all dressed up as reasonableness.

You will find this phrase lurking in:

- Subcontractor approvals
- Assignment or novation clauses
- Requests for access to site or information
- EOT agreement provisions
- Variation approvals
- Subletting or personnel changes

It sounds fair. But it creates asymmetric discretion:

- The Employer holds the right.
- The Contractor bears the burden to prove delay, obstruction, or bad faith.

LEGAL INSIGHT:

In *Gan Insurance Co Ltd v Tai Ping Insurance Co Ltd*[20] [2001] EWCA Civ 1047, the Court of Appeal confirmed that a power to withhold consent is not a licence for arbitrary refusal. Where consent is required and cannot be unreasonably withheld, the refusal must be connected to the contractual purpose and supported by commercially rational grounds.

In *Porton Capital Technology Funds v 3M UK Holdings Ltd*[21] [2011] EWHC 2895 (Comm), the court confirmed that refusal may still be reasonable even where it frustrates the requesting party, provided it is grounded in legitimate commercial interests. In practice, "reasonable" does not mean helpful, quick, or cooperative. It means defensible.

---

20 Gan Insurance Co Ltd v Tai Ping Insurance Co Ltd [2001] EWCA Civ 1047, United Kingdom (Court of Appeal).

21 Porton Capital Technology Funds v 3M UK Holdings Ltd [2011] EWHC 2895 (Comm), United Kingdom (Commercial Court).

WHERE THIS UNDERMINES ENTITLEMENT

Scenario:

- You request a variation.
- Employer delays consent for 4 weeks
- You cannot proceed.
- They claim you should have "taken steps" anyway.

Your delay claim?
At risk, because they never said "no," just… *not yet.*
And their refusal?
Cloaked behind "commercial justification" that may not withstand scrutiny.

HOW TO FIX IT:

Always tie "consent" to:

- A defined response timeframe
- A default escalation path if silent

Example fix:

"Consent shall not be unreasonably withheld or delayed. Where no response is provided within five working days, the request shall be deemed escalated to the Engineer under Clause X.X."

Or:

"Refusal must be accompanied by written justification."

This puts burden and transparency back into the clause.

WTF SCORING SYSTEM™

Metric	Score
WTF Factor	9.0/10 – Polite Permission Trap
Risk Profile	HIGH – Employer discretion, Contractor consequence
Verdict	DEFINE deadlines & escalation or AVOID if possible

ENGINEERING TAKEAWAY:

'Consent shall not be unreasonably withheld' is no safety: it's a wait with an easy out!

Set a time limit for answers!

"The contract never forgets your mistakes—only who made them first."

– Jinoy's Law on Contract Memory

"Your silence gives consent." – Plato

CLAUSE #13

"Any omission shall not be construed as a waiver..."

aka: *The Clause That Pretends It Was Watching All Along*

ENGINEER'S TRANSLATION:

"We said nothing. But we still have the right to punish you. Retroactively."

SATIRICAL INTERPRETATION:

This clause is the contractual equivalent of a poker face.

It means:

"Just because we did not enforce it, does not mean we forgot. Or forgave. Or agreed."

It lets the Employer:

- Ignore a breach.
- Say nothing for weeks.
- And still come back later to say:

"You were in default. We just did not mention it."

It is the legal version of:
"I saw everything. I was just waiting."

WHY THIS IS A PROBLEM:

This clause preserves the Employer's rights even when they do nothing. It says silence is not consent, omission is not waiver, and failure to act does not mean you can rely on it. In effect, it turns every unspoken issue into a live wire, ready to shock you later.

This clause is used to:

- Keep rights alive even after silence.
- Protect against accidental waiver.
- Allow retroactive enforcement of LDs, terminations, or rejections.

It is common in:

- Default clauses
- LD provisions
- Completion acceptance clauses
- Notice enforcement
- Payment dispute timelines

The problem?

It keeps the Employer's power "active" even when they are passive.
You think the issue was accepted.
You relied on that silence.
You moved on. They moved the goalposts. And now you are paying for the game they said nothing about.
Then they issue a retroactive rejection, deduction, or notice, and point to this clause as the reason.

LEGAL INSIGHT:

Non-waiver clauses are useful, but they are not magic. In *Tele2 International Card Company SA v Post Office Ltd*[22] [2009] EWCA Civ 9, the Court of Appeal confirmed that a party may still lose the right to terminate where its conduct amounts to an election to affirm the contract, even where a non-waiver clause exists.

The practical lesson is simple: silence may not automatically waive a right, but prolonged inaction, continued performance, or conduct inconsistent with enforcement can still create serious risk. This clause is therefore stronger than assumption, but weaker than certainty. It preserves rights on paper, but conduct can still destroy them in practice.

HOW THIS CLAUSE HURTS ENGINEERS & CLAIMS

You think:

- They did not object to your programme
- They approved the delay event.
- They accepted the material spec by silence.

Then at final account or arbitration:

"We never waived our right to reject that. See Clause 21.9."

You are blindsided because this clause creates a one-sided memory.

HOW TO FIX IT:

Add boundaries or triggers to its use. For example:

"This clause shall not apply where the omission continued beyond 28 days without written objection."

Insert mutuality:

---

22 Tele2 International Card Company SA v Post Office Ltd [2009] EWCA Civ 9, United Kingdom (Court of Appeal).

"Neither Party shall be deemed to have waived its rights by omission unless such omission continues without correction or reservation for a period exceeding X days. Nothing in this clause shall prevent the Contractor from raising an estoppel defence where it has relied in good faith on the Employer's prolonged silence, and such reliance caused material prejudice."

Reinforce with estoppel protection:

"Nothing in this clause shall preclude a finding of reliance where one party acted in good faith based on the other party's silence."

WTF SCORING SYSTEM™

Metric	Score
WTF Factor	9.1/10 – Silent Authority Retained
Risk Profile	HIGH – Delayed enforcement trap
Verdict	CONDITION or QUALIFY with timeline & reliance exception

ENGINEERING TAKEAWAY:

If silence means nothing,
And acting means everything,
Then you are always one step away from being retroactively wrong.

Construction Lessons Series 006

> *"The surest sign a job is finished is when the Employer discovers a new beginning."*

"It's not dead, it's just resting." – Monty Python

CLAUSE #14

"This clause shall survive termination..."

***aka:** The Zombie Clause That Never Dies*

ENGINEER'S TRANSLATION:

"The contract may end. But this clause will haunt you long after."

SATIRICAL INTERPRETATION:

This is the **undead clause** of construction contracts.

You terminate the Agreement. You leave the site. You close the final account.
And then this clause taps you on the shoulder and says:
"Not so fast."

It is the contractual version of:
"I may be gone, but I'm not done."

WHY THIS IS A PROBLEM:

This clause refuses to die with the contract. It revives itself after termination to demand deliverables, assert obligations, and impose liabilities, long after you thought the relationship was over. If left unchecked, it becomes the ghost clause that haunts your final account.

You will find this phrase attached to:

- Confidentiality clauses
- Indemnities
- Dispute resolution obligations.
- IP rights
- Limitation of liability clauses
- Continuing obligations in novation or subcontracts

At first glance, it seems protective.

But when written broadly or lazily, it allows:

- Open-ended liability
- Unenforceable obligations post-termination
- Conflict with limitation periods or dispute resolution time bars

LEGAL INSIGHT:

Termination does not automatically erase every contractual consequence. In *Photo Production Ltd v Securicor Transport Ltd*[23] [1980] AC 827, the House of Lords confirmed that termination for breach does not necessarily destroy clauses which govern the consequences of that breach. Some obligations may continue because they are expressly preserved or because they are necessary to deal with accrued rights, liability, confidentiality, indemnity, or dispute resolution.

In *Heyman v Darwins Ltd*[24] [1942] AC 356, the House of Lords recognised that an arbitration clause may survive termination for the purpose of resolving disputes arising out of the contract. The danger is not survival itself. The danger is vague survival: a clause that continues without saying what survives, for how long, and for what purpose.

---

23 Photo Production Ltd v Securicor Transport Ltd [1980] AC 827, United Kingdom (House of Lords).

24 Heyman v Darwins Ltd [1942] AC 356, United Kingdom (House of Lords).

WHERE THIS BECOMES A CLAIMS NIGHTMARE

Say you terminate the contract.

You believe your obligations have ceased.

Then the Employer says:

"Ah, but Clause 27.5 survives. And under that clause, you owe us an updated set of BIM models, full as-built drawings, and all warranties certified by a third party."

You are now doing unpaid work for a contract that no longer exists.

HOW TO FIX IT:

Specify which clauses survive, not just "this clause."

"Clauses X.X (Confidentiality), X.X (Indemnity), and X.X (IP Rights) shall survive termination."

Define a duration:

"...for a period not exceeding 12 months post-termination unless otherwise agreed."

Ensure it **does not conflict** with limitation periods or statute of repose.

Be especially cautious when used in **subcontracts**, you may outlive the main contractor's obligations.

WTF SCORING SYSTEM™

Metric	Score
WTF Factor	9.0/10 – Clause That Refuses to Die
Risk Profile	HIGH – Endless exposure post-contract
Verdict	LIMIT by scope & duration or DEFINE specific survival rights

ENGINEERING TAKEAWAY:

Some obligations must continue.

But if your clause is still working after your contract has died, that is not commitment. That is possession.

Set clear end dates.

Construction Lessons Series 007

> *"Progress meetings exist chiefly to demonstrate that progress is impossible."*

"The beatings will continue until morale improves." – Naval Proverb

CLAUSE #15

"The Contractor Shall Not Be Entitled To Any Additional Cost or Time..."

aka: *The Clause That Cancels Your Entire Claim (Almost)**

ENGINEER'S TRANSLATION:

"Whatever happens, deal with it.
You signed it.
Now build it."

SATIRICAL INTERPRETATION:

This clause is the legal version of:
"Do not complain. Do not delay. Do not even think about being paid more."
It is often used as a catch-all exclusion to eliminate even legitimate claims.

You ask:
"What if the delay came from the Employer?"
Clause says: No time. No cost.
You ask:

"What if the variation was massive?"
Clause says: Still no time. Still no cost.
It is the default setting for Employer absolution.

WHY THIS IS A PROBLEM:

This clause shuts the door before you even knock. It pre-emptively denies entitlement to cost or time, no matter the cause. Whether it is a change, a disruption, or an Employer-induced delay, the clause says: "Don't ask. We already said no."

This clause appears in:

- Variation conditions
- Force majeure exclusions
- Design coordination disclaimers.
- Interface delay carve-outs.
- Lump sum pricing provisions

It seems to protect against trivial claims, but it often ends up eliminating valid ones, including:

- Employer-caused delays
- Unexpected cost shocks
- Disruptive access sequences
- Critical design change impacts

Even when the Employer is at fault, this clause allows them to reject all claims unless specific carve-outs exist.

LEGAL INSIGHT:

In *North Midland Building Ltd v Cyden Homes Ltd*[25] [2018] EWCA Civ 1744, the Court of Appeal upheld clear wording which allocated the risk of concurrent delay to the Contractor, even where an Employer-risk event was also operating.

---

25 North Midland Building Ltd v Cyden Homes Ltd [2018] EWCA Civ 1744, United Kingdom (Court of Appeal).

The decision confirms that courts may enforce express risk allocation where the wording is clear, even if the result is commercially harsh.

Gaymark Investments Pty Ltd v Walter Construction Group Ltd[26] [1999] NTSC 143 is often cited as a contrasting approach, where Employer-caused delay and strict notice machinery contributed to a time-at-large outcome. It should be treated as a jurisdiction-specific warning, not as the English position. The lesson is simple: a "no cost, no time" clause may survive if clearly drafted, but it must be tested against the EOT mechanism, prevention risk, and the governing law.

HOW THIS SHOWS UP IN CLAIM DISMISSALS

You submit a delay claim based on:

- Late IFC drawings
- Conflicting site access
- Client-side rework
- Impossible sequencing

Response?

"Clause 12.9 of the Contract clearly states: 'The Contractor shall not be entitled to any additional cost or time on account of...'"

And just like that, your detailed claim becomes a footnote.

HOW TO FIX IT:

Never accept **unqualified** exclusions.

Recast the clause with specific boundaries:

"Except where such delay or cost is caused by the Employer or arises from a Change Order under Clause X.X..."
Use fair risk-sharing language:

26 Gaymark Investments Pty Ltd v Walter Construction Group Ltd [1999] NTSC 143, Australia (Supreme Court of the Northern Territory).

"This clause shall not apply to events outside the Contractor's reasonable control or where the Employer's instructions are materially responsible."
Alternatively, insert:

"Notwithstanding this clause, the Contractor shall remain entitled to relief in accordance with Clauses X.X (EOT), X.X (Variation), or X.X (Force Majeure)."

WTF SCORING SYSTEM™

Metric	Score
WTF Factor	9.4/10 – Entitlement Eraser
Risk Profile	CRITICAL – Kills valid cost/time claims
Verdict	REWRITE to qualify or CROSS-REFER relief clauses

ENGINEERING TAKEAWAY:

If a clause says, "no cost and no time", it usually means no claim, no negotiation, and no way out.

Unless you fix it first.

"Assumption is the mother of all mistakes." – Military Proverb

CLAUSE #16

"The Contractor Shall Be Deemed to Have Satisfied Himself…"

***aka:** The Clause That Makes You Psychic at Tender Stage*

ENGINEER'S TRANSLATION:

"You have seen the site, read the specs, met the team, and predicted the future. You've no excuses now."

SATIRICAL INTERPRETATION:

This clause pretends you are clairvoyant.

It assumes you knew:

- The quality of the buried soil strata
- The Hydrological Data at 12m depth
- The exact position of the undocumented utilities
- And that the Employer would never issue final IFCs on time

And if you did not?
Unless contractually qualified, the phrase 'deemed to have satisfied' may shift unforeseen risks to the Contractor, even if such conditions were undisclosed, concealed, or materially misleading at the time of tender.

This is the contractual version of:
"We already gave you a chance to complain. You just did not realise it."

WHY THIS IS A PROBLEM:

This clause grants you hindsight liability at tender stage. By "deeming" you to have satisfied yourself, it transforms unknowns into assumptions and surprises into negligence. You are not just building the project; you are retroactively liable for predicting it.

You will find this clause buried in:

- Site condition disclaimers
- Access risk allocations
- Tender declarations
- "No claim" statements tied to data room or pre-bid inspections.

It works by:

- Shifting risk without evidence
- Blocking entitlement for unforeseen site or interface conditions
- Deeming knowledge you never had as your contractual baseline.

This clause weaponises hindsight against you.

This clause shall not apply where the Contractor's reliance was based on documents provided by the Employer that were materially misleading or incomplete.

LEGAL INSIGHT:

In *Tharsis Sulphur & Copper Co v McElroy & Sons*[27] (1878) 3 App Cas 1040, the House of Lords held that a contractor who undertook to satisfy himself as to the site conditions could not later recover merely because the conditions proved more difficult than expected. The risk had been contractually assumed.

---

27 Tharsis Sulphur & Copper Co v McElroy & Sons (1878) 3 App Cas 1040, United Kingdom (House of Lords).

The danger is not inspection itself. The danger is legal fiction. A "deemed to have satisfied himself" clause can convert limited tender access into full risk acceptance unless it is qualified. Contractors should preserve express carve-outs for latent conditions, incomplete or misleading Employer information, undisclosed risks, and matters not reasonably discoverable at tender stage.

WHERE THIS KILLS LEGITIMATE CLAIMS

You hit:

- Unforeseen soil collapse
- Missing permissions
- Critical drawing errors
- Differing site levels

You submit a claim.

Employer says:

"Clause 3.1.4: 'The Contractor shall be deemed to have satisfied himself as to the site conditions, information adequacy, and access risks.'"

Just like that, you are claiming against a clause that already pre-dismissed you.

HOW TO FIX IT:

Narrow the clause:
"The Contractor shall satisfy himself to the extent information provided is reasonably available and not materially misleading."
Or:
"This clause shall not limit the Contractor's right to claim for conditions materially differing from site data provided or for undisclosed Employer risks."

Insert this in tender Q&A:
"Bidders are not deemed to have assessed latent conditions or incomplete design packages."

This creates a clear risk boundary.

WTF SCORING SYSTEM™

Metric	Score
WTF Factor	9.3/10 – Hindsight Clause in Disguise
Risk Profile	CRITICAL – Total bar on legitimate claims
Verdict	QUALIFY or EXCLUDE in sensitive conditions

ENGINEERING TAKEAWAY:

If you are "deemed to know everything" at tender stage, then you are already liable for everything that went wrong.

Before you even mobilised. Ask for clear site data now or you will be blamed for every problem.

"If you start work without approval, it's initiative. If you wait, it's delay."

– Jinoy's law on variations

"Better three hours too soon than a minute too late." – Shakespeare

CLAUSE #17

"No Claim Shall Be Entertained Unless..."

aka: *The Time Bar Trapdoor Clause*

ENGINEER'S TRANSLATION:

"You are entitled to claim. But only if you speak up fast enough, and in the exact way we like."

SATIRICAL INTERPRETATION:

This clause is not about rejecting your entitlement. It is about saying:

"You missed the deadline to tell us that you were entitled."

It turns procedure into a weapon, where:

- The quality of your delay does not matter.
- The fairness of your case does not matter.
- Only the timing and formatting of your notice matters

It is the legal version of:

"It does not matter that you were right. It matters that you missed a 14-day deadline, while the client was 14 weeks late. And now, the entire claim file goes in the shredder, because—yes, Clause 20.1 says so."

WHY THIS IS A PROBLEM:

This clause weaponizes timing over merit. It turns the notice procedure into a landmine, where one missed date or wrong recipient can destroy an otherwise valid claim. You may be right, but if you are late, the contract says you are wrong.

This clause is often found in:

- Notice of delay provisions
- Variation time limits
- Force majeure declarations
- Final account or claims closing language.
- Termination dispute timeframes

It gives the Employer a procedural firewall.

Even if your claim is valid, it can be rejected because:

- You sent the notice on Day 15 instead of Day 14
- You emailed the PM but not the Engineer.
- You submitted delay particulars, but not "within the format set out in Appendix A."

LEGAL INSIGHT:

In *Multiplex Construction (UK) Ltd*[28] *v Honeywell Control Systems Ltd* [2007] EWHC 447 (TCC), the court confirmed that notice provisions expressed as conditions precedent can be enforced where the contract clearly states the consequence of non-compliance. A valid delay or variation claim may therefore fail if the required notice is late, defective, or sent through the wrong contractual route.

Gaymark Investments Pty Ltd[29] *v Walter Construction Group Ltd* [1999] NTSC 143 is often cited as a contrasting Australian decision, where Employer-caused

---

28 Multiplex Construction (UK) Ltd v Honeywell Control Systems Ltd [2007] EWHC 447 (TCC), United Kingdom (Technology and Construction Court).

29 Gaymark Investments Pty Ltd v Walter Construction Group Ltd [1999] NTSC 143, Australia (Supreme Court of the Northern Territory).

delay and strict notice machinery contributed to a time-at-large result. It should be treated as a jurisdiction-specific warning, not as the English default. The lesson is blunt: a time-bar clause is not a discipline tool. It is a guillotine with a calendar attached.

WHERE THIS TRIGGERS CLAIM COLLAPSE:

Scenario:

- You notify a 60-day critical path delay.
- Impact is evident.
- But you submitted the notice 2 days late due to ongoing negotiation.

Response?
"Rejected under Clause 20.1: no claim shall be entertained unless written notice was provided within 14 days of the event."

No discussion. No consideration. Just rejection.

HOW TO FIX IT:

Add "reasonableness" to the clause:

"Unless the delay in notification did not materially prejudice the Employer's ability to investigate the event..."

Or create a fallback:

"Late notice may be accepted subject to mutual agreement or if the delay event is ongoing or not reasonably discoverable within the notice period."

And always make the notice requirements clear, who, when, how.

WTF SCORING SYSTEM™

Metric	Score
WTF Factor	9.5/10 – Procedural Guillotine
Risk Profile	CRITICAL – Kills otherwise valid claims
Verdict	INSERT RELIEF language or TIE to PREJUDICE, not formality alone

ENGINEERING TAKEAWAY:

You can be right.
You can be delayed.
You can be ready to prove it.

But if you are late by one clause, you lose everything.

Construction Lessons Series 008

"Honesty in claims is like sunshine on site—everyone likes the idea of it."

"Obey first, complain later." – Military Adage

CLAUSE #18

"The Contractor Shall Proceed with the Works Notwithstanding any Dispute..."

***aka:** The Clause That Silently Kills Your Right to Object*

ENGINEER'S TRANSLATION:

"Do what we say now. Complain later if you can still afford to."

SATIRICAL INTERPRETATION:

This clause says:

"Build first. Argue later. And maybe never."

It is the contractual equivalent of a magic trick:

- The Employer instructs a variation or change.
- You follow it under protest.
- Then later they say:

"We never agreed that was a variation.
Clause 21.3 says you had to proceed regardless."
Now you are chasing time, cost, and documentation **after the fact**, while being told:
"You did it voluntarily."

WHY THIS IS A PROBLEM:

This clause demands obedience first, discussion later. It insists you proceed "notwithstanding" disagreement, documentation gaps, or financial risk, while quietly undermining your ability to recover cost or time. You stay compliant, but you get punished.

You will find this clause in:

- Variation and instruction procedures
- Dispute escalation frameworks.
- Design change directions.
- Emergency response clauses
- Acceleration instructions

It sounds operational.
It encourages continuity.

But it is often used to:

- Silence contractor hesitation
- Avoid formal agreement before impact is incurred.
- Weaken variation claims post-execution.

LEGAL INSIGHT:

"Proceed notwithstanding dispute" clauses are usually enforced because projects cannot stop every time entitlement is contested. But performance alone does not preserve recovery. The Contractor must proceed while also protecting its position through timely notice, clear protest, valuation records, and express reservation of rights.

In *Multiplex Construction (UK) Ltd v Honeywell Control Systems Ltd*[30] [2007] EWHC 447 (TCC), the court confirmed that contractual notice machinery can operate as a condition precedent to entitlement. In *Henry Boot Construction*

30 Multiplex Construction (UK) Ltd v Honeywell Control Systems Ltd [2007] EWHC 447 (TCC), United Kingdom (Technology and Construction Court).

Ltd v Alstom Combined Cycles Ltd[31] [2005] EWCA Civ 814, the Court of Appeal confirmed that payment rights may depend on the contractual certification machinery, not merely on the fact that work was performed. The lesson is simple: obedience keeps the project moving; paperwork keeps the claim alive.

HOW THIS TRIGGERS ENTITLEMENT COLLAPSE

Scenario:

- The Engineer issues verbal instruction: "Proceed with cable rerouting."
- You ask for written confirmation. They quote Clause 13.7:

"The Contractor shall proceed with the Works notwithstanding any disagreement as to entitlement."

- You proceed. Variation claim denied. They argue:

"You did the work. There was no disagreement at the time. And you did not notify us properly."

You are now both compliant and unpaid.

HOW TO FIX IT:

Never accept this clause without paired safeguards.

Example amendment:

"The Contractor shall proceed, provided that doing so does not waive any right to cost or time relief under Clause X.X. Written notice of such intent shall be submitted within 7 days."

Or:

"Proceeding under protest shall not prejudice the Contractor's entitlement, provided timely notice is served in accordance with Clause X.X."

---

31 Henry Boot Construction Ltd v Alstom Combined Cycles Ltd [2005] EWCA Civ 814, United Kingdom (Court of Appeal).

Include the phrase:
"Proceeding shall not constitute Agreement."

WTF SCORING SYSTEM™

Metric	Score
WTF Factor	9.3/10 – Perform Now, Dispute Later (If You Dare)
Risk Profile	HIGH – Undermines variation and delay claims
Verdict	REWRITE with notice protection or ADD NON-WAIVER language

ENGINEERING TAKEAWAY:

If you are told to "just proceed," do not assume you will be paid for it. Because a clause that keeps you compliant may also keep you powerless.

Construction Lessons Series 009

"Authority expands to occupy every silence in the contract."

"Art is never finished, only abandoned." – Leonardo da Vinci

CLAUSE #19

"All Documents Shall Be Prepared in a Form Acceptable to the Employer…"

aka: *The Never-Ending Redline Clause*

ENGINEER'S TRANSLATION:

"You will submit. They will comment. You will revise. Repeat until morale breaks."

SATIRICAL INTERPRETATION:

This clause is how **drawings become Groundhog Day**.

You revise the as-built. They say, *"Please update formatting."*
You update formatting. They say, *"Please adjust the legend."*
You adjust the legend. They say, *"Not acceptable, resubmit in A1 and A3."*

And when you ask what "acceptable" means?

They smile and say:
"You will not get a checklist. You'll get feedback like: Make it more formal but simpler. And shrink it to A1 and A3 and, no, not like that."

WHY THIS IS A PROBLEM:

This clause turns document control into a game of endless redlines. "Form acceptable to the Employer" becomes an undefined moving target, allowing rejection without reason, delay without fault, and late certification without consequence.

This clause appears in:

- As-built drawing obligations
- Test certificates
- Method statements
- HSE plans
- Close-out documents
- Pre-construction design deliverables

It sounds reasonable.
But "acceptable to the Employer" gives unbounded discretion.

That means:

- No timeline for review
- No objective approval criteria
- No limit to the number of rejections

LEGAL INSIGHT:

A requirement that documents be in a form "acceptable" to the Employer gives the Employer an evaluative discretion. In *Socimer International Bank Ltd v Standard Bank London Ltd*[32] [2008] EWCA Civ 116, the Court of Appeal confirmed that such discretion must be exercised honestly, in good faith, and without arbitrariness, capriciousness, perversity, or irrationality.

But that does not give the Contractor an easy remedy. Where the contract defines no acceptance criteria, rejection is rarely simple to attack unless bad faith, irrationality, or departure from the contractual purpose can be shown.

---

32 Socimer International Bank Ltd v Standard Bank London Ltd [2008] EWCA Civ 116, United Kingdom (Court of Appeal).

An undefined standard of "acceptability" gives one party a veto without accountability and turns document approval into a loop with no finish line.

WHERE THIS DAMAGES REAL PROJECTS

Close-out deadline looms. You submit final handover documents. Employer redlines minor formatting. They delay certification. LD clock keeps ticking.

You protest, but the contract says:
"All documents must be in a form acceptable to the Employer."

So even if 99% is complete, you are technically non-compliant. Subjectivity in document 'acceptance' is not just inefficient; it is financially destructive.

HOW TO FIX IT:

Define "acceptability" as tied to:

- Compliance with specification
- Format standards agreed during project start.
- Objective quality criteria

Example clause:

"Documents shall be deemed acceptable if they conform to the Contract Requirements, including formatting and content specified in Appendix X."

Impose procedural boundaries:

"The Employer shall respond within seven working days. Failure to respond shall constitute deemed acceptance."

Always insert:

"Approval shall not be unreasonably withheld or delayed."

WTF SCORING SYSTEM™

Metric	Score
WTF Factor	9.0/10 – Deliverable on a Loop
Risk Profile	HIGH – Delays certification and creates LD risk
Verdict	DEFINE acceptability or TIME-LIMIT approval process

ENGINEERING TAKEAWAY:

When "acceptable" is undefined, you are resubmitting until they run out of objections, not until you meet a standard. Set clear finish lines now.

"It's not you, it's me." – Cliché

CLAUSE #20

"Nothing in this Agreement Shall Be Construed as Creating a Partnership…"

aka: *The Clause That Wants Distance, Until There's a Dispute*

ENGINEER'S TRANSLATION:

"We will work together. We will collaborate. We will coordinate.
But if this goes sideways, you are on your own."

SATIRICAL INTERPRETATION:

This is the **"it's not a relationship" clause** of contracting.
You share plans. You attend joint meetings. You defend each other's claims.

Then the dispute hits.
You reach out for support. And the other side says:
"There is a clause. It says we are not partners. Good luck."

It is like co-signing a mortgage and then saying:
"We were just friends."

WHY THIS IS A PROBLEM:

This clause is often inserted to protect against unintended legal consequences, but it cannot override how the parties actually behave. Even when expressly denying partnership, if your commercial conduct indicates shared control, joint risk, or cooperative decision-making, courts may infer a de facto partnership regardless of the wording. That makes this clause more about optics than immunity, and dangerously misleading if your actions say otherwise.

This clause shows up in:

- Joint venture agreements
- Consortium or alliance contracts
- Design-build team arrangements.
- EPC partnerships
- Engineering service + execution hybrids

It is meant to avoid:

- Joint liability
- Fiduciary duty
- Tax exposure as a "partnership."

But if the behaviour on the project looks like a partnership, courts might treat it as one, clause or not.

LEGAL INSIGHT:

A "no partnership" clause is useful, but it is not a complete substitute for consistent conduct. Courts look at substance as well as wording: whether the parties shared profit, exercised joint control, represented themselves jointly, or carried on business together.

In *Khan v Miah*[33] [2000] 1 WLR 2123, the House of Lords confirmed that a partnership may arise once parties begin carrying on business with a view to profit, even before formal trading has begun. The lesson is simple: if the contract says "no partnership" but the project behaviour suggests joint

33 Khan v Miah [2000] 1 WLR 2123, United Kingdom (House of Lords).

business, shared control, or common risk, the clause may reduce the argument, but it may not end it.

WHERE THIS BACKFIRES HARD

In a dispute:

- Your JV partner withheld client communication.
- You get pulled into arbitration as co-defendant.
- You argue: "We had no legal link. See the 'no partnership' clause."
- Tribunal says: *"Yes, but you co-signed letters, shared risk, and made joint decisions. That is enough."*

So now the clause did not save you but gave you false security.

HOW TO FIX IT:

Be specific, not sweeping. Replace generic language with:

"This Agreement does not constitute a partnership under the Partnership Act 1890 or any fiduciary or agency relationship unless explicitly stated in Clause X.X."

List exclusions AND cooperative intent separately:

"Each party remains independent, and no joint liability shall arise except where expressly agreed under Clause X.X (e.g., joint indemnities or dispute submissions)."

Align behaviour with wording, no shared bank accounts, no joint letterheads, no client-side decisions made jointly without clarity.

To avoid inadvertent partnership: avoid joint bank accounts, shared indemnities, or jointly signed project representations.

WTF SCORING SYSTEM™

Metric	Score
WTF Factor	8.7/10 – Cold Until It is Convenient
Risk Profile	HIGH – Denies liability, implies unity
Verdict	DEFINE exceptions or ALIGN language with conduct

ENGINEERING TAKEAWAY:

If you act like partners, spend like partners, and defend like partners, a clause alone cannot save you from the partnership you pretended not to have.

"Responsibility behaves like gravity—it always falls on the Contractor."

– Jinoy's law on Risk Transfer

"Responsibility without control is the fastest route to bankruptcy." – Unknown

CLAUSE #21

"The risk Shall Remain with the Contractor Until the Issue of the Taking Over Certificate…"

aka: *The Clause That Makes You Insurable Until the End, And Then Liable Again*

ENGINEER'S TRANSLATION:

"You have finished the work. Everyone is using it. But until we issue a piece of paper, you still carry all the risk."

SATIRICAL INTERPRETATION:

You built it. They are operating it. You have demobilised.
But the clause says:
"Until we officially tell you we've taken over, you still own it."

This clause turns completion into a legal illusion. You think risk passed with performance.

But this clause says:
"Risk passes with paperwork."

WHY THIS IS A PROBLEM:

This clause delays the moment risk actually transfers from the Contractor to the Employer, not when the work is done, tested, or even being used, but only when a formal certificate is issued. That disconnect between performance and paperwork exposes the Contractor to liability long after control has been lost.

This clause appears in:

- FIDIC Red, Yellow, and Silver Book models
- EPC main contracts
- Offshore, oil & gas, and utility projects.
- Any contract with formal *Taking Over Certificates (TOC)* or *Sectional Completions*

It sounds procedural, but it:

- Delays risk transfer beyond actual delivery.
- Makes you liable for third-party use, Employer-caused damage, or operational mishaps after you leave site.
- Leaves you exposed even when you have no control over the asset.

LEGAL INSIGHT:

Where the contract clearly states that risk remains with the Contractor until formal Taking Over, courts and tribunals will usually begin with that wording. Actual completion, successful testing, or Employer use may not be enough if the contract makes certification the trigger for risk transfer.

In *MT Højgaard A/S v E.ON Climate & Renewables UK*[34] [2017] UKSC 59, the Supreme Court reinforced that clear contractual obligations can be enforced even where the Contractor has performed and believes it has complied. Applied here, the danger is not completion. The danger is the gap between completion and certification. If risk moves only when paper is issued, the Contractor may remain exposed after control has already passed in practice.

---

34 MT Højgaard A/S v E.ON Climate & Renewables UK [2017] UKSC 59, United Kingdom (Supreme Court).

WHERE THIS GOES WRONG IN REAL LIFE

You complete the works.
The Employer starts using the plant.
Commissioning succeeds.

But the Engineer delays the Taking Over Certificate for "administrative reasons."
Then a third-party damages the installed works.

Insurance refuses to pay because:

- "It was operational."
- "It was not under your control."
- "The policy does not clearly match the contract's risk-transfer date."

But the contract says:

"Risk remains with the Contractor until TOC."
Now you are exposed, but powerless.

HOW TO FIX IT:

Clarify what triggers risk transfer:
"Risk shall transfer to the Employer upon Substantial Completion or first beneficial use of the Works by the Employer, whichever occurs earlier, notwithstanding any delay in the issuance of the Taking Over Certificate."

Separate legal risk from operational risk:
"The Contractor shall not be liable for third-party damage after physical handover, unless due to Contractor default."

Insert default TOC trigger:
"If no TOC is issued within 14 days of handover, risk shall be deemed transferred."

This prevents paperwork-based liability extensions.

WTF SCORING SYSTEM™

Metric	Score
WTF Factor	9.2/10 – Completion Without Protection
Risk Profile	HIGH – Post-performance liability trap
Verdict	LINK to practical use or INSERT auto-trigger clause

ENGINEERING TAKEAWAY:

You can finish the work.
You can pass every test.
But if they do not sign the TOC,
You still own the risk.

Without the asset.

Construction Lessons Series 010

"Experience is the name contractors give to what the Engineer rejected last time."

"No good deed goes unpunished." – Clare Boothe Luce

CLAUSE #22

"The Subcontractor Shall Be Bound to the Contractor in the Same Manner as the Contractor is Bound to the Employer..."

***aka:** The Clause That Copies and Pastes Your Misery Downstream*

ENGINEER'S TRANSLATION:

"If I suffer, you suffer. No exceptions. No edits. No explanation."

SATIRICAL INTERPRETATION:

This clause is copy-paste delegation at its finest.

The Contractor says:
"Whatever the Employer makes me suffer, I now pass to you."

It sounds efficient. But what it really says is:
"You are now bound by a contract you have never read, in full, at your own risk."

It is the contractual version of:
"Trust me. It is all in there somewhere."

WHY THIS IS A PROBLEM:

On paper, it sounds like flow-down simplicity. In reality, it transfers undefined obligations to a Subcontractor without full disclosure, adequate access to the Main Contract, or any procedural clarity, creating liability through implication.

This clause is a staple of back-to-back contracts, especially in:

- MEP, façade, and specialist subcontracting
- Lump sum or unit rate sub-agreements
- Mega-project EPC models
- JV-led or fast-tracked programmes

It creates a "flow-down" obligation, but often without:

- Full disclosure of the Main Contract
- Alignment of scope, deadlines, or procedures
- Clarity on rights, caps, time bars, or EOT relief

LEGAL INSIGHT:

Back-to-back wording does not work by atmosphere. In *Mouchel Ltd v Van Oord UK Ltd*[35] [2011] EWHC 72 (TCC), the court examined the actual allocation of design, workmanship, and responsibility under the relevant contracts rather than treating liability as automatically transferred by broad wording. The lesson is that flow-down risk must be specific, incorporated, and workable.

If a Contractor wants to pass Main Contract obligations downstream, the relevant obligations must be identified, incorporated, and made workable within the Subcontract.

---

35 Mouchel Ltd v Van Oord UK Ltd [2011] EWHC 72 (TCC), United Kingdom (Technology and Construction Court).

General phrases such as "in the same manner" may signal an intention to pass risk downstream, but they do not automatically reproduce every notice period, claims procedure, dispute route, cap, exclusion, or entitlement mechanism. A "same manner" clause is not a mirror. It is a fog that hides whose risk is really being carried.

WHERE THIS EXPLODES

Scenario:

- Employer imposes 5-day notice for variations.
- Subcontract only says: "Subcontractor shall be bound in same manner..."
- Subcontractor not informed.
- Contractor's claim rejected for late notice.
- Subcontractor's pass-through claim also denied because no direct compliance clause exists.

Everyone loses.

Because "in the same manner" means nothing if procedures are not mirrored.

HOW TO FIX IT:

Replace vague references with specific ones:
"The Subcontractor shall comply with Clauses 20.1, 20.2, and 13.3 of the Main Contract, as set out in Appendix X."

Provide access to the Main Contract or extract relevant clauses.
Or add a protection clause:
"Where time or procedural obligations are passed down, the Contractor shall notify the Subcontractor within sufficient time to enable compliance."

Never assume that *"same manner"* = *same obligation.* It rarely does.

WTF SCORING SYSTEM™

Metric	Score
WTF Factor	9.1/10 – Back-to-Back Booby Trap
Risk Profile	HIGH – Undefined flow-down liabilities
Verdict	IDENTIFY SPECIFIC CLAUSES or DISCLOSE FULL FLOW-DOWN TERMS

ENGINEERING TAKEAWAY:

If you are asked to accept someone else's contract without seeing it, you are not a subcontractor.

You are a contractual ghostwriter for someone else's liability. Ask to see it all!

Construction Lessons Series 011

"The longer the report, the shorter the truth."

"If you want to make God laugh, tell him your plans." – Woody Allen

CLAUSE #23

"The Employer Shall Have the Right to Assign this Agreement without Consent..."

aka: *The Clause That Changes the Game Without Warning*

ENGINEER'S TRANSLATION:

"You thought you knew who you were working for? Surprise!
It is someone else now, and you have no say."

SATIRICAL INTERPRETATION:

This clause is like someone swapping business cards halfway through dinner.

You build trust, negotiate payment schedules, navigate site politics.

Then suddenly you receive a letter saying:
"As of today, your contract is now with XYZ Real Estate Holdings (SPV-92)."

No conversation. No negotiation. Just legal teleportation.

WHY THIS IS A PROBLEM:

This clause allows the Employer to unilaterally assign the Agreement, replacing your counterparty without consultation or consent. The result? You could find yourself tied to an unknown entity with no recourse, no commercial history, and no security of performance.

This clause appears in:

- EPC and developer-side main contracts
- Concession-based infrastructure projects
- PPP/PFI and private equity-driven build-operate agreements.
- Real estate and asset-backed contracts

It allows the Employer to:

- Transfer the contract to a third party (often SPVs or funders)
- Without your consent
- Without renegotiation
- While retaining all your obligations exactly as is

And if the new party is:

- Insolvent
- Hostile
- In a jurisdiction you cannot enforce against…

You are stuck. Because you agreed to deal with whoever holds the paper, not who you signed with.

LEGAL INSIGHT:

Assignment clauses are governed by their wording. In *Linden Gardens Trust Ltd v Lenesta Sludge Disposals Ltd*[36] [1994] 1 AC 85, the House of Lords confirmed that contractual restrictions on assignment can be effective where clearly drafted. The same logic cuts both ways: if the contract clearly permits

36 Linden Gardens Trust Ltd v Lenesta Sludge Disposals Ltd [1994] 1 AC 85, United Kingdom (House of Lords).

assignment, the Contractor may find itself bound to perform for a different counterparty without fresh negotiation.

The danger is not assignment itself. The danger is assignment without safeguards. If the assignee lacks financial standing, operational capacity, decision-making continuity, or enforceable security, the Contractor's risk changes even though the written obligations remain the same.

WHERE THIS DESTROYS PREDICTABILITY

You agreed to collaborate with a reputable developer.

Three months in, the Employer assigns the contract to:

- A shell holding company.
- A distressed fund
- A newly formed JV partner with no operational presence

You now have:

- No payment security
- No visibility into decision-makers
- No continuity on design approvals or prior commitments

And when you object?

The reply is:
"Clause 1.9: The Employer may assign this Agreement without consent."

In cross-border projects, unconsented assignments may shift jurisdictional enforcement rights, especially dangerous in SPV-based developments.

HOW TO FIX IT:

Require **consent for assignment**, or at least notification with recourse.
"The Employer may assign this Agreement only upon prior written notice to the Contractor, provided the assignee has equivalent financial standing, assumes the Employer's payment and performance obligations, and provides equivalent security."

Alternatively:
"Assignment shall not affect accrued rights, project approvals, or agreed payment milestones."

Include:
"The Contractor shall have the right to suspend performance if assignment creates material risk to payment or delivery."

WTF SCORING SYSTEM™

Metric	Score
WTF Factor	9.0/10 – Surprise Party With New Risk
Risk Profile	HIGH – Contract may be transferred to unknown entity
Verdict	INSERT consent/condition or DEFINE recourse rights

ENGINEERING TAKEAWAY:

Contracts are not relationships.
You do not get to pick the new party after the switch.
So make sure the clause gives you a seat at the table before it is too late.

"The single biggest problem in communication is the illusion that it has taken place."
– G.B. Shaw

CLAUSE #24

"In the Event of Conflict, the English Version Shall Prevail..."

aka: *The Clause That Forgot You Are in a Non-English-Speaking Country*

ENGINEER'S TRANSLATION:

"This is a bilingual contract. But if anything goes wrong, just assume your language does not count."

SATIRICAL INTERPRETATION:

This clause pretends to respect both languages.
But really, it whispers:
"We printed your version to be polite. Ours is the one that matters."

So when a dispute arises about timing, scope, or LDs;
The Employer pulls out the English version and says:
"This is the real contract. The other one was just for reference."

It is the linguistic equivalent of:
"We heard you. We just did not mean it."

WHY THIS IS A PROBLEM:

Despite claiming to resolve conflicts in multilingual contracts, this clause often collapses under the weight of local legal systems. Courts may override it in favour of statutory language preferences, making your "prevailing language" clause a false sense of security.

This clause appears in:

- Government or semi-government contracts in GCC, LATAM, North Africa, or Asia
- FIDIC-based frameworks adapted for dual-language regions.
- Infrastructure, energy, and PPP contracts executed under non-English legal systems.

The problem?

- Local courts often default to the native language of the Governing Law
- Arbitrators may be forced to compare interpretations line by line.
- Key clauses, especially termination, delay, variation, and LDs, can shift meaning dramatically depending on syntax.

In *several* unreported cases, contractual clauses, interpreted in English were reversed in GCC courts, due to Arabic version weight under local law, despite the "English prevails" clause.

LEGAL INSIGHT:

A clause stating that the English version shall prevail may create interpretive certainty between the contracting parties, but it does not automatically override the procedural law of the forum, mandatory court-language rules, official translation requirements, or statutory protections in non-English jurisdictions.

The real risk is not that English cannot be chosen. It often can. The risk is assuming that a priority clause will control every forum in every situation. In local courts, public authority dealings, labour filings, licensing, tax, customs, or administrative proceedings, the operative language may be determined by law, not by drafting preference. Language priority clauses protect contractual confidence; they do not replace local-law compliance.

WHERE THIS CAUSES CHAOS

Your contract has English and say, Arabic texts.
The Employer terminates you under Clause 15.2.

In English:

"The Employer may terminate for cause with 14 days' notice."

In Arabic:
"The Employer may terminate without compensation if the Contractor delays."

You go to local court. The court applies the local-language version or the official translation.
Your English clause is overridden. Now the clause that "protects you" becomes a translation trap.

HOW TO FIX IT:

Add this safeguard to the clause:
In the event of any inconsistency between language versions, both versions shall be interpreted to reflect the shared commercial intent of the Parties; where a conflict remains, the English version shall prevail for the purposes of international arbitration, save where prohibited by applicable mandatory law.

During negotiation, have both versions legally validated, not just translated.

WTF SCORING SYSTEM™

Metric	**Score**
WTF Factor	9.1/10 – Translation Without Protection
Risk Profile	HIGH – Clause may collapse under jurisdictional challenge
Verdict	ALIGN with local law or VALIDATE both versions as binding

ENGINEERING TAKEAWAY:

Contracts may be written in English.
But if the court only reads Arabic, Chinese, French, or Spanish;
Your clause might as well be invisible. Check local laws now!

"Design by Employer, blame the Contractor—the circle of contractual life."

– Jinoy's Law on Construction Design

"Responsibility without power—the worst of all positions." - Churchill

CLAUSE #25

"The Contractor Shall Be Fully Responsible for the Design, Notwithstanding Any Review or Comment By the Engineer…"

aka: *The Clause That Pretends the Review Was Just for Fun*

ENGINEER'S TRANSLATION:

"You must design it. We will review it. But if it fails, it is your fault. Even if we told you, it was fine."

SATIRICAL INTERPRETATION:

This clause is a masterclass in selective memory & responsibility.
It says: *"We'll review your design, ask you to change it, possibly delay it, and then deny any accountability."*

It turns the Engineer into a:

- Critic with no consequence
- Commenter without co-liability
- Delayer without responsibility.

It is like being handed exam papers back with teacher comments, then being failed for following them.

WHY THIS IS A PROBLEM:

This clause retains the Contractor's full design liability, even when the Engineer has reviewed, commented on, or approved the design. It neutralises the review process, offering no protection or shared accountability, turning every approval into a potential trap.

This clause appears in:

- EPC and Design-Build contracts
- D&B subcontracts and novated design consultant scopes
- Hybrid D&C models where the Employer or Engineer "retains right to review."

The clause's danger lies in this combination:

- You carry 100% of design liability.
- They keep full right to review, comment, and reject.
- But their feedback has no legal weight.

LEGAL INSIGHT:

In *MT Højgaard A/S v E.ON Climate & Renewables UK*[37] [2017] UKSC 59, the Supreme Court confirmed that a contractor may remain bound by clear design and performance obligations even where it has followed specified standards or received Employer-side input. Compliance with review procedures does not, by itself, transfer design risk.

---

37 MT Højgaard A/S v E.ON Climate & Renewables UK [2017] UKSC 59, United Kingdom (Supreme Court).

In *London Borough of Merton v Lowe (Builders) Ltd*[38] (1981) 18 BLR 130, the court treated design responsibility as following the party responsible for the design decision, not merely the party who reviewed or commented on it. Applied here, Engineer review is not the same as Engineer assumption of liability. Unless the comment amounts to a binding design instruction or materially alters the design basis, the Contractor may still carry the design risk.

WHERE THIS BACKFIRES ON CONTRACTORS

You submit design.
Engineer reviews.

They say: "Approved with minor comments."
You proceed.
It fails during operation.
Claim filed against you.

You say:
"But it was reviewed and accepted."
They say:
"Clause 6.2.4 – Contractor is fully responsible notwithstanding any review."

Suddenly, you are carrying the consequence of a design you co-developed, but they get a free pass.

HOW TO FIX IT:

Insert carve-outs:

"The Contractor shall remain responsible for design, except where the Engineer's review requires a departure from good industry practice or imposes specific instructions that override the Contractor's original intent."

Or:

---

38 London Borough of Merton v Lowe (Builders) Ltd (1981) 18 BLR 130, United Kingdom (Court of Appeal).

"Where Engineer comments materially alter the design basis, such change shall be documented and liability shared."

Always document protests to impractical review comments before implementation.

WTF SCORING SYSTEM™

Metric	Score
WTF Factor	9.2/10 – Design Approval with Zero Responsibility
Risk Profile	CRITICAL – Full liability despite external interference
Verdict	QUALIFY Engineer's review or LIMIT LIABILITY where design is overridden

ENGINEERING TAKEAWAY:

If you design it, you own it. But if they change it, and you still own it, that is not risk allocation.

That is delegated sabotage.

Construction Lessons Series 012

"Common sense always turns up late to the kick-off meeting."

"Bureaucracy defends the status quo long past the time the quo has lost its status."
– L.J. Peter

CLAUSE #26

"The Contractor Shall Obtain All Necessary Approvals, Permits, and Licences…"

aka: *The Clause That Makes You Responsible for Bureaucracy You Cannot Control*

ENGINEER'S TRANSLATION:

"You need to get approvals.
From authorities you do not control.
Within timelines they do not follow.
Using formats they do not publish."

SATIRICAL INTERPRETATION:

This clause hands you a to-do list, walks away, and then sets a countdown clock. It says:

"You are responsible for obtaining all permits, even when the authority is on holiday, the forms are in triplicate, and the approving Engineer's cousin just got married in the Ministry."

It is like being told:

"You must deliver on time. And also, please coordinate with an unpredictable entity who responds in astrological cycles."

This clause assumes:

- You have the authority of a government.
- The influence of a lobbyist
- And the patience of a monk

You do not. Yet you are still liable.

WHY THIS IS A PROBLEM:

This clause assigns you the responsibility for navigating a bureaucratic maze; one with no map, no timeline, and no guarantee of exit. It assumes you control authorities you cannot influence; and makes you liable for delays you cannot prevent. This clause is standard in:

- Mobilisation and site access provisions
- Environmental and utility coordination
- Authority approvals for design, inspection, handover
- Health, safety, and fire compliance procedures

The danger? It assigns responsibility without power.

So if the:

- Municipality delays your NOC.
- Fire authority reschedules your inspection.
- Building permit takes 3 weeks longer than "usual"
  ...you pay the price. In time and in LDs.

This clause makes you accept that risk in one sentence.

LEGAL INSIGHT:

A permit obligation is enforceable if the contract clearly allocates it. The difficulty is not the duty to apply; it is the risk of delay caused by authorities the Contractor does not control. Unless the clause separates application responsibility from approval risk, the Contractor may be liable for government delay, inspection rescheduling, or administrative inaction despite having taken all reasonable steps.

The safer drafting distinction is simple: the Contractor may be responsible for preparing, submitting, and diligently pursuing applications within its control, but time relief should remain available where delay is caused by the authority, Employer-held information, missing Employer approvals, or statutory processes outside the Contractor's control.

WHERE THIS CLAUSE EXPLODES

You plan mobilisation. You apply for the gate pass. The Labour Ministry holds your paperwork for 9 days.

Then the Engineer says:
"Why are you late?"
You explain. They point to Clause 4.5:

"The Contractor shall obtain all necessary permits, approvals, and licences..."

The Employer, of course, has relationships with the authorities. You have... Google Translate and your PRO's uncle's brother in Law.

And now you are 9 days late, for reasons you could not control.

HOW TO FIX IT:

Add a cooperation clause:
"The Employer shall provide all information, signatures, access, authorisations, and statutory support reasonably required for permits that depend on Employer cooperation or authority action."

Insert force majeure language for unreasonable delay:
"Permits delayed due to government inaction shall entitle the Contractor to time relief."

Define boundaries:

"This obligation excludes permits designated as Employer obligations under Appendix X." And most critically:

Tie risk to influence, not ownership.

WTF SCORING SYSTEM™

Metric	Score
WTF Factor	9.1/10 – Full Responsibility, No Authority
Risk Profile	HIGH – Delays caused by third parties, paid for by you
Verdict	INSERT shared obligation or EXCLUDE uncontrollable authorities

ENGINEERING TAKEAWAY:

You cannot control the Ministry. You cannot force approvals.

But this clause pretends you can, then blames you when it all falls apart.

Construction Lessons Series 013

"Fairness in a contract is the optimism of the first draft."

"If you're early, you're on time; if you're on time, you're late." – Coaching Proverb

CLAUSE #27

"Time and Date Shall Be of the Essence in Respect of All Obligations Under this Agreement..."

aka: *The Clause That Thinks It's a Stopwatch, not a Contract*

ENGINEER'S TRANSLATION:

"Every date is critical. Every delay is fatal. Even if it was just a coffee break."

SATIRICAL INTERPRETATION:

This clause is a performance-enhancing drug for the legal team.

It turns your entire contract into a high-speed pursuit, where every minute counts, every form matters, and every delay is a breach.

You missed a notice deadline by two hours?
"Time is of the essence. Welcome to the breach."

This clause does not just take schedule seriously; it takes it personally.

It is what happens when a lawyer reads a Gantt chart and decides to weaponise the calendar.

WHY THIS IS A PROBLEM:

This clause takes the calendar and turns it into a weapon. Every timeline becomes a trap; every missed submission becomes a breach; every procedural slip becomes material default. It confuses urgency with unforgiveness; and it grants no grace, no flexibility, no sense. This clause is often found in:

- Notice requirements
- Variation response deadlines
- Payment processing windows
- Programme submissions
- Completion and handover obligations

It overrides commercial proportionality by saying:

"Every deadline is essential. No grace. No flexibility. No common sense."

Where time is made "of the essence," any delay, however small, constitutes breach unless waived. Time-critical clauses may be enforceable where they are strictly expressed as essential.

Which means:

- Forget 14-day EOT claim triggers.
- Forget minor delays in programme delivery.
- Forget waiting for that design approval before you mobilise.

With this clause, every delay is treated like it ruined the project.

LEGAL INSIGHT:

In *Bremer Handelsgesellschaft mbH*[39] *v Vanden Avenne Izegem PVBA* [1978] 2 Lloyd's Rep 109, the House of Lords emphasised the importance of clear wording where a time requirement is intended to operate as a condition precedent. If missing the deadline is intended to destroy entitlement, the contract should say so plainly.

39 Bremer Handelsgesellschaft mbH v Vanden Avenne Izegem PVBA [1978] 2 Lloyd's Rep 109, United Kingdom (House of Lords).

In *Bunge Corp*[40] *v Tradax Export SA* [1981] 1 WLR 711, the House of Lords treated a time stipulation in a mercantile contract as a condition, allowing termination where notice was given late. The lesson for construction is not that every late memo becomes fatal. The lesson is that if time is made essential for every obligation, even minor procedural delays can be converted into alleged default unless the clause is limited to genuinely time-critical obligations.

WHERE THIS KILLS COMMON SENSE

You submit your programme 24 hours late.
No impact on site.
No delay to material orders.

The Employer says:
"Time is of the essence in respect of all obligations. You are in material breach."

You scramble. Lawyer pulls out Clause 4.1(e).
Suddenly your EOT entitlement is suspended, not for delay, but for delay in paperwork.

HOW TO FIX IT:

Narrow the clause:
"Time shall be of the essence solely with respect to the Completion Date and milestone obligations specified in Appendix X."
Add commercial sanity:
"Time shall be of the essence except where delay is minor, procedural, or does not materially impact project performance."

Always separate:

- Time-critical dates (handover, access, commissioning)
- From procedural dates (responses, submittals, reports)

40 Bunge Corp v Tradax Export SA [1981] 1 WLR 711, United Kingdom (House of Lords).

This clause should not apply to everything, especially not notice windows or mid-week memos.

WTF SCORING SYSTEM™

Metric	Score
WTF Factor	9.3/10 – Stopwatch Mentality Meets Liquidated Damages
Risk Profile	HIGH – Makes every deadline a landmine
Verdict	RESTRICT scope or APPLY only to key dates

ENGINEERING TAKEAWAY:

A schedule is not a sacred text.
Not every date is life or death.

But this clause? It makes every breath a breach.

"There are known knowns and known unknowns..." – Donald Rumsfeld

CLAUSE #28

Apparently, I priced this too.

"The Contractor Shall Be Deemed to Have Allowed for All Risks in his Price..."

aka: *The Clause That Converts Lump Sum into Lump Regret*

ENGINEER'S TRANSLATION:

"If anything goes wrong, it was your fault for not pricing it. Even the things we forgot to tell you."

SATIRICAL INTERPRETATION:

This is the clause that assumes you are a contractual clairvoyant.

It says:
"If the wind changes, if the Client changes, if the drawings contradict themselves, it is all in your price."

You thought you submitted a bid.
Turns out you also priced climate change, geopolitical instability, and every inconsistency in the Employer's data room.

This clause takes your BOQ and turns it into a blank cheque, with your name on the bottom.

WHY THIS IS A PROBLEM:

This clause rewrites your contract with invisible ink. You thought you priced what was shown; this clause says you priced what was missing. It converts your bid into a confession; and makes your contingency a scapegoat for every unknown. You will find this tucked into:

- Lump sum commercial clauses
- Tender disclaimers
- Employer's scope notes
- Risk allocation appendices.

Its goal?
To kill variation claims, EOTs, and cost relief in one line.

The clause removes your right to say:

"We did not know." "This was not included." "This was changed after award."

It answers all three with:
"Tough. You priced all risks."

LEGAL INSIGHT:

In *Mitsui Construction Co Ltd v Attorney General of Hong Kong*[41] [1986] 33 BLR 1, the Privy Council examined whether the contract truly allocated the risk of materially different ground conditions to the Contractor. The court resisted an interpretation that would turn a major public works contract into a substantial commercial gamble unless the wording clearly required that result.

Applied here, the danger is the word "all". If the contract clearly identifies the risks included in the price, the Contractor may be held to that bargain. But a vague statement that the Contractor has allowed for "all risks" should not be treated as a magic eraser for Employer changes, undisclosed information, contradictory documents, or risks that could not reasonably have been priced at tender.

---

41 Mitsui Construction Co Ltd v Attorney General of Hong Kong [1986] 33 BLR 1, Hong Kong (Privy Council).

WHERE THIS WRECKS YOUR CLAIM

The Employer changes 30% of the scope post-award.
You raise a variation.

They say:
"Clause 14.7: The Contractor is deemed to have priced all risks."

You say:
"That change came after award!"

They reply:
"You priced uncertainty. It is called contingency."
Now you are in a variation dispute **without a variation.**

HOW TO FIX IT:

Limit the clause:

"The Contractor shall be deemed to have allowed for risks listed in Appendix Y. Other risks shall be compensated in accordance with Clause X.X (Variation)."

Define risk types:

"This clause excludes Employer-responsible delays, design changes, and unknown site conditions."

Remove "all" entirely:

"The Contractor has priced standard risks associated with execution, excluding extraordinary or post-award events."

Because no one can price for everything, especially not the unknown.

WTF SCORING SYSTEM™

Metric	Score
WTF Factor	9.4/10 – Insurance Without the Insurance
Risk Profile	CRITICAL – Wipes out entitlement before it begins
Verdict	QUALIFY OR DELETE or LIST known risk categories only

ENGINEERING TAKEAWAY:

If you are "deemed" to have allowed for all risks, then you are not bidding.

You are being set up.

"The only thing more permanent than concrete
is the Contractor's liability for it."

– Jinoy's Law on Liability

"The palest ink is better than the best memory." – Chinese Proverb

CLAUSE #29

"No Oral Agreement or Representation Shall Be Binding..."

aka: *The Clause That Deletes Your Entire Kick-Off Meeting*

ENGINEER'S TRANSLATION:

"Whatever was said, agreed, confirmed, promised, or understood, if it was not typed and signed, it never happened."

SATIRICAL INTERPRETATION:

This clause is the legal version of selective amnesia.

It says:

"That meeting you had? That call? That WhatsApp message? Lovely conversation. Zero legal value."

You may have:

- Agreed on revised scope.
- Got a verbal go-ahead to proceed.
- Confirmed a change with three witnesses.

But unless someone wrote it down on company letterhead and signed in blue ink, this clause considers it hallucination.

It is the contractual equivalent of:
"Pictures or it didn't happen and in this age of AI...."

WHY THIS IS A PROBLEM:

This clause strips words of value and meetings of meaning. It pretends conversations did not happen; instructions do not count; field agreements were figments of your imagination. It is a legal eraser for human understanding. This clause lives in:

- Entire Agreement clauses
- Closing boilerplate sections
- Contract signature blocks.
- Employer-friendly amendments to standard forms

It appears harmless, just a neat "wrap-up" clause. But it:

- Invalidates verbal instructions.
- Blocks claims based on field agreements.
- Wipes out pre-contract understandings.

LEGAL INSIGHT:

In *Inntrepreneur Pub Co v East Crown Ltd*[42] [2000] 2 Lloyd's Rep 611, the court upheld the commercial purpose of an entire agreement clause: to prevent parties later relying on stray pre-contract statements, informal assurances, or alleged collateral promises that were not included in the written contract.

In *AXA Sun Life Services plc v Campbell Martin Ltd*[43] [2011] EWCA Civ 133, the Court of Appeal confirmed the limit of that approach. A basic entire agreement

42 Inntrepreneur Pub Co v East Crown Ltd [2000] 2 Lloyd's Rep 611, United Kingdom (High Court).

43 AXA Sun Life Services plc v Campbell Martin Ltd [2011] EWCA Civ 133, United Kingdom (Court of Appeal).

clause may exclude collateral warranties or prior contractual promises, but it will not necessarily exclude liability for misrepresentation unless the wording clearly says so. The lesson is simple: if oral instructions or representations matter, record them properly before they become legally invisible.

WHERE THIS NULLIFIES REAL ENTITLEMENTS

The Client says during kickoff:
"We'll send you the formal variation later, go ahead and start."

You proceed.
Six weeks later, you submit the claim.

They say:
"Clause 21.10: No oral representation shall be binding. You proceeded at your own risk."

You realise you are being billed for taking their word seriously.

HOW TO FIX IT:

Add a softening clause:

"Oral agreements shall be documented in writing within 5 days. Failure to do so shall not automatically invalidate the agreement where both parties acted upon it."

Insert reliance logic:

"This clause shall not exclude reliance on verbal instructions where actions were visibly taken in consequence and documented contemporaneously."

And most importantly:

- Log everything
- Follow up in writing.
- Never trust memory where clauses act like document shredders.

Courts may still recognise estoppel where reliance and detriment are clearly proven, but the evidentiary burden is high and rarely met without contemporaneous records.

WTF SCORING SYSTEM™

Metric	Score
WTF Factor	9.3/10 – Gaslight in Legal Font
Risk Profile	HIGH – Voids handshake deals, field decisions
Verdict	QUALIFY OR REMOVE or ADD reliance protection

ENGINEERING TAKEAWAY:

If your contract says nothing spoken is binding, then you better have a keyboard, a timestamp, and a paper trail.

Because your word is not worth the clause it was excluded by.

Construction Lessons Series 014

"Payment certificates travel slower than bad news."

"The most terrifying words: I'm from the government and I'm here to help." – Reagan

CLAUSE #30

"The Employer May Terminate for Convenience at Any Time…"

aka: *The Clause That Makes You Disposable by Clause 18.3*

ENGINEER'S TRANSLATION:

"We can end this contract whenever we like.
You cannot."

SATIRICAL INTERPRETATION:

This is the "it's not you, it's us" clause, only with invoices still unpaid and 202 site workers in limbo.

It says:
"We hired you. We used you. But we have changed direction. Kindly demobilise. Oh, and you may not be entitled to anything except what we want to give you."

You think you are in a relationship. The clause says:
"You are a subscription. We can cancel anytime."

It is the legal equivalent of ghosting, just with more paperwork.

WHY THIS IS A PROBLEM:

This clause turns commitment into a coin toss. It allows the Employer to end the contract not for breach, not for cause, but for preference. You mobilise, invest, and perform; they walk away; and you are left to sweep up the loss.

You will find this clause lurking in:

- Main contractor agreements with developers
- Government and semi-government contracts
- EPC contracts under political or uncertain funding
- Fast-tracked projects with shifting scopes

Its purpose?

To give the Employer a built-in exit strategy, no matter how far along you are, or how much you have invested.

Which usually means:

- No lost profits
- No demobilisation costs
- No commercial goodwill

LEGAL INSIGHT:

Termination for convenience clauses may be enforceable where the contract clearly gives one party that right and defines the consequences of its exercise. The commercial problem is not termination itself; it is termination without a complete compensation mechanism.

In *Abbey Developments Ltd v PP Brickwork Ltd*[44] [2003] EWHC 1987 (TCC), the court examined the use of contractual powers to remove work and the consequences of doing so. The case illustrates the wider construction-law point: if the Employer is allowed to withdraw work or end performance for convenience, the contract should state clearly what becomes payable, including

44 Abbey Developments Ltd v PP Brickwork Ltd [2003] EWHC 1987 (TCC), United Kingdom (Technology and Construction Court).

work done, demobilisation, procurement commitments, subcontractor liabilities, and any agreed margin. A convenience clause without payment machinery is not flexibility. It is an exit door with the invoice left behind.

In some civil-law and Middle Eastern jurisdictions, termination rights may also be tested against good faith, abuse of rights, or mandatory statutory controls. The governing law therefore matters: a convenience clause that is enforceable in one forum may attract closer scrutiny in another.

WHERE THIS LEAVES YOU HANGING

You mobilise. You set up site.
You place long-lead orders.
Then comes the email:
"Clause 19.4 invoked. This contract is terminated for convenience. Submit your account."

You submit. They reject:

"Only completed and certified works will be paid. Clause 21.3(b)."

You now have idle labour, stranded equipment, and a P&L that reads like a horror story.

HOW TO FIX IT:

Require minimum notice period:
"Termination for convenience shall be subject to 30 days' written notice and payment of all properly incurred costs up to the effective date of termination, including demobilisation, committed procurement, subcontractor cancellation costs, and agreed margin on work removed."

Insert recovery for lost margin:
"The Contractor shall be entitled to profit on works removed by termination, subject to valuation under Clause X.X."

List payable cost heads:

- Material offloading
- Demobilisation
- Restocking fees
- Subcontractor settlements

Otherwise, the clause terminates your rights along with your contract.

WTF SCORING SYSTEM™

Metric	Score
WTF Factor	9.2/10 – Ghosted by Clause
Risk Profile	HIGH – Work removed without justification or compensation
Verdict	CONDITION with notice & cost or REMOVE entirely unless justified

ENGINEERING TAKEAWAY:

If your contract says they can walk away anytime, make sure you are not the one left footing the bill.

Convenience for them should not mean consequences for you.

Construction Lessons Series 015

"Lawyers invented ambiguity so engineers wouldn't feel lonely."

"Too many cooks spoil the contractor." – Parody

CLAUSE #31

"The Contractor Shall Ensure No Disruption to Other Contractors..."

aka: *The Clause That Assumes You Control the Entire Site*

ENGINEER'S TRANSLATION:

"You must coordinate everyone on site. Except... you have no authority, no information, and no power to tell them anything."

SATIRICAL INTERPRETATION:

This clause thinks you run the site like a military base. In reality, you are:

- Just one contractor
- In a swarm of others
- All armed with cherry pickers, cranes, excuses, and claims

Yet this clause makes you accountable for disruption by:

- The plumbing subcontractor three tiers below
- The scaffolding team you have never met.
- The lift installer whose schedule was drawn in invisible ink.

It is like being told:
"Please keep the whole school quiet. But you are only the Class Monitor"

WHY THIS IS A PROBLEM:

This clause demands that you manage an entire site you do not control; coordinate people you do not employ; and prevent disruption from teams whose names you do not even know. It gives you blame without authority; and responsibility without power. You will find this clause in:

- Site coordination and sequencing sections
- Temporary works and mobilisation appendices
- Safety and productivity obligations
- EPC interface clauses with multiple work fronts

The problem?

- No reciprocal obligation from the others
- No enforcement power
- No defined coordination plan

The clause imposes strict coordination responsibility on the Contractor without granting sitewide control, programme authority, or enforcement levers. It offends the commercial logic that responsibility should follow control.

This clause dumps the responsibility, but not the tools.

LEGAL INSIGHT:

A coordination obligation is enforceable, but it should be matched with the authority needed to perform it. If the Contractor is required to prevent disruption by others, the contract should also give access to the master programme, advance notice of other contractors' activities, coordination authority, interface procedures, and a route to relief where disruption is caused by parties outside the Contractor's control.

In *Costain Ltd v Bechtel Ltd*[45] [2005] EWHC 1018 (TCC), the court examined the importance of contractual role, authority, and decision-making power in project administration. Applied here, the principle is practical:

45 Costain Ltd v Bechtel Ltd [2005] EWHC 1018 (TCC), United Kingdom (Technology and Construction Court).

responsibility for site coordination should follow control. A clause that imposes accountability without programme authority, access information, or enforcement power turns cooperation into blame.

WHERE THIS GOES WRONG IN REAL LIFE

You follow your programme. You start the ceiling works. HVAC contractor shows up unannounced and blocks scaffold access.

They log a disruption. The PM says:
"Clause 6.4: You were responsible for not interfering with others."

You explain you had no notice of their work.

They reply:
"Not our problem. You were supposed to ensure coordination."

Now you are both delayed and liable.

HOW TO FIX IT:

Add mutual coordination clause:

"Contractor shall coordinate its activities reasonably with other contractors, where such contractors are identified in the Employer's Master Programme and under direct Employer control."

Insert dependency protections:

"The Contractor shall not be held liable for disruption caused by third parties outside its contractual control or work interface."

Clarify limits:

"Responsibility for coordination is limited to parties directly engaged under this Contract or whose works are scheduled under Appendix Y."

If you are going to be the site marshal, give yourself the whistle.

WTF SCORING SYSTEM™

Metric	Score
WTF Factor	9.0/10 – Blame Without Authority
Risk Profile	HIGH – Liability for others' behaviour
Verdict	ADD interface plan or QUALIFY with control limits

ENGINEERING TAKEAWAY:

You can manage your team. You can coordinate your scope.

But this clause assumes you can orchestrate the entire site, like a conductor with no baton.

"Give me a lever long enough, and I will move your liability." – Archimedes Parody

CLAUSE #32

"The Contractor Shall Indemnify the Employer Against Any and All Losses..."

aka: *The Clause That Has No Upper Limit and No Expiry Date*

ENGINEER'S TRANSLATION:

"If anything goes wrong, ever, you are paying for it. Whether it was your fault, someone else's, or an act of God."

SATIRICAL INTERPRETATION:

This clause says:
"If there is damage, we blame you. If there is delay, we bill you. If there is doubt, we invoice you."

It is not an indemnity clause. It is a contractual black hole. Once signed, all liability is gravitationally pulled toward you.

Forget capped liability. Forget proportionate fault. This clause says:
"All losses. Any amount. Forever."

It is the legal equivalent of:
"Whatever happens, you are paying. Even if we caused it. Even if it happened on a different project."

WHY THIS IS A PROBLEM:

This clause writes a blank cheque against your future; it indemnifies the Employer for everything, whether or not you caused it; whether or not you knew it; whether or not it makes commercial sense. It is not insurance; it is exile. You will find this clause in:

- Indemnity and liability sections
- Employer-favoured subcontract templates
- Risk transfer provisions in EPC and design-build agreements.
- Force majeure back doors disguised as indemnity clauses.

Its tricks include:

- No financial cap
- No causation requirement
- No time limitation
- No fault link

This clause may be challenged if it omits caps, causation, or carve-outs. Tribunal would view it as commercially unreasonable and in breach of contra proferentem principles.

This clause does not shift liability, it dumps a truckload of liability in your front yard, with no forwarding address.

LEGAL INSIGHT:

In *Shell UK Ltd v Total UK Ltd*[46] [2010] EWCA Civ 180, the court reminded us that indemnity clauses must be construed strictly, especially where they are used to shift broad financial consequences. Clear words matter because indemnities can move liability beyond ordinary damages.

---

46 Shell UK Ltd v Total UK Ltd [2010] EWCA Civ 180, United Kingdom (Court of Appeal).

In *Transocean Drilling UK Ltd*[47] *v Providence Resources plc* [2016] EWCA Civ 372, the Court of Appeal enforced a sophisticated commercial risk-allocation regime, confirming that broad indemnity and consequential loss wording may be effective where the drafting is clear. The lesson is not that wide indemnities fail automatically. The lesson is worse: they may work. A clause covering "any and all losses" must therefore be tied to fault, causation, defined loss categories, caps, exclusions, and expiry.

WHERE THIS BECOMES FINANCIAL SUICIDE

A subcontractor damages a fire pump.

It halts commissioning for 2 days.

The Employer files a claim for:

- Lost revenue
- Reputational damage
- Additional security staff
- Extra bottled water for visitors

You say:

"We were not at fault."

They say:
"Clause 16.2: You indemnify us against all losses arising from the Works."

You now owe more than you billed, for someone else's mistake.

HOW TO FIX IT:

Cap liability:
"Contractor shall indemnify the Employer for direct losses arising solely from the Contractor's negligence or breach. Indemnity capped at Contract Price or insurance value."

---

47 Transocean Drilling UK Ltd v Providence Resources plc [2016] EWCA Civ 372, United Kingdom (Court of Appeal).

Tie to fault:
"Indemnity shall apply only to losses arising directly from the Contractor's negligence, breach, or wilful misconduct."

Define exclusions:
"This indemnity shall not cover indirect, consequential, or Employer-caused losses."

Insert expiry:
"Indemnity obligation shall lapse 24 months after Taking Over Certificate."

Otherwise, you have signed a clause that is part liability… part eternity.

WTF SCORING SYSTEM™

Metric	Score
WTF Factor	9.5/10 – Infinite Liability Simulator
Risk Profile	CRITICAL – Total financial exposure, no fault needed
Verdict	CAP & LINK TO FAULT, STRIKE, OR REWRITE COMPLETELY

ENGINEERING TAKEAWAY:

An indemnity should protect, not punish.

But if your clause covers "any and all losses," you just agreed to fund problems you did not cause… on someone else's contract.

"If a clause can be read two ways, the Employer meant the expensive one."

– Jinoy's Law on Contract Ambiguity

"Out of sight is out of scope." – Adapted Proverb

CLAUSE #33

"The Contractor Shall Not be Entitled to Rely on Any Documents Not Listed in Appendix X…"

aka: *The Clause That Pretends the Data Room Never Existed*

ENGINEER'S TRANSLATION:

"You saw drawings. You based your bid on them. We even discussed them. But they are not listed here, so now they do not exist."

SATIRICAL INTERPRETATION:

This clause is a magician's trick: It makes evidence disappear with footnotes.

It says:
"Unless it is listed in this appendix, it never influenced your bid, it was never relied upon, and it shall never be used against us."

The entire pre-award data room? Gone.
The Q&A clarifications? Vanished.
The preliminary drawings you priced. Now irrelevant.

This is legal gaslighting, documented.

WHY THIS IS A PROBLEM:

This clause deletes your reality and replaces it with a table of contents. It says: if a document is not listed, it does not exist, no matter how clearly you relied on it; no matter how decisively it shaped your price; no matter how consistently it guided your work. The clause strips the Contractor of pre-contract reliance rights unless the Employer properly lists documents.

This clause hides in:

- Contract document hierarchies.
- Scope confirmations
- Tender disclaimers
- Appendices listing "Contract Documents"

Its goal? To deny your right to rely on:

- Pre-contract site data
- Employer-issued "for information only" drawings
- Clarification meetings
- Tender addenda not reissued formally.

This clause takes that principle, and weaponises it.

LEGAL INSIGHT:

Contract documents are not remembered by fairness. They are remembered by incorporation. If a document is not included in the contract list, order of precedence, appendix, tender addendum, or agreed clarification record, the party relying on it may face a serious evidential and contractual hurdle.

The danger is not that unlisted documents are always irrelevant. The danger is that the contract may allow the Employer to argue that they were never part of the bargain. Data-room documents, tender clarifications, preliminary drawings, and "for information" material should therefore be expressly incorporated, excluded, or ranked. If the contract memory is selective, your claim may become invisible.

WHERE THIS UNDERMINES YOUR ENTIRE CLAIM

You priced based on:

- Rev-B architectural drawings
- Tender Q&A responses
- Technical clarifications from the bid stage

Later, the Employer says:
"Clause 1.4: Contractor shall not rely on any document not listed in Appendix X."
You check Appendix X:

- BOQ
- Specs
- General Conditions

Your documents? Not there.
Now your price is "unsupported,"
Your scope "was misunderstood,"

And your EOT is "not substantiated."

HOW TO FIX IT:

Incorporate key references:
"All documents issued during the tender process and formally relied upon in pricing shall be deemed incorporated unless expressly excluded."

Add a fallback:
"Where documents materially influenced the pricing or design intent and were issued by the Employer, they shall be deemed included."

List types, not just titles:
"All IFC drawings, pre-contract clarifications, and formally issued correspondence shall form part of the Contract Documents."

If your contract can forget, you must remember to document.

WTF SCORING SYSTEM™

Metric	Score
WTF Factor	9.2/10 – Document Amnesia Clause
Risk Profile	HIGH – Nullifies priced scope and justifications
Verdict	INCLUDE all relied documents or DEFINE "Contract documents" explicitly

ENGINEERING TAKEAWAY:

If a clause pretends your documents never existed, your price becomes fiction, and your claim becomes a ghost story.

Construction Lessons Series 016

"Every miracle on site begins with a typo in the drawing."

"Weekends are just weak ends." – Aphorism

CLAUSE #34

"Any Reference to 'Day' Means Calendar day…"

aka: *The Clause That Hates Weekends, Holidays, and Site Realities*

ENGINEER'S TRANSLATION:

"The deadline includes Sundays, Eid, Diwali, National Day, your site shutdown, and your son's birthday. Tick tock."

SATIRICAL INTERPRETATION:

This clause thinks a day is a day is a day.
It says:
"We do not care if it is a public holiday, a Friday in the Gulf, or the day after a cyclone. If it is on the calendar, it counts."

You missed a submission by one day?
"It was a Sunday? Not our problem. Clause 20.3 says 'calendar day.'"

This clause turns your carefully built claim timeline into a legal speedrun, with no pit stops, no long weekends, and definitely no Christmas grace.

It is the contractual equivalent of:
"Deadline falls on a public holiday. Celebrate faster."

WHY THIS IS A PROBLEM:

This clause must accommodate real-world project rhythms. Enforcing short deadlines over religious holidays, lock downs, or declared site closures may create practical unfairness unless the clause provides a clear extension mechanism. This clause counts days like machines count seconds. It gives no pause for holidays; no grace for shutdowns; no recognition that real projects live in real calendars with non-working days.

You will see this clause in:

- Time-bar provisions
- Variation notification clauses
- Programme update schedules.
- Submittal response timelines

It is meant to be "clear," but it creates:

- Unrealistic deadlines
- Missed notices.
- Triggers for breach when no office was even open.

LEGAL INSIGHT:

A contract may define "day" as calendar day, and courts will usually start with the wording the parties chose. The danger is not the definition itself. The danger is applying it blindly to short procedural windows, especially where the deadline falls across weekends, holidays, site shutdowns, or authority closures.

In *Education 4 Ayrshire Ltd*[48] *v South Ayrshire Council* [2009] CSOH 146, the court treated contractual notice machinery seriously in a construction project context. The lesson is practical: if the contract says calendar days, assume the clock runs unless the clause expressly extends time for non-working days, public holidays, or office closures. Calendar certainty is useful. Calendar ambush is not.

---

48 Education 4 Ayrshire Ltd v South Ayrshire Council [2009] CSOH 146, Scotland (Outer House, Court of Session).

WHERE THIS SHUTS DOWN YOUR ENTITLEMENT

You receive a formal instruction on a Thursday.
Your contract says:
"Notify of any claim within 7 calendar days."

You calculate:

- Day 1 = Friday
- Day 2 = Saturday
- Day 3 = Sunday
- Day 4–7 = site closed, Eid holidays

You submit on Day 8. Response?
"Clause 17.4 breached. Notification window closed."

You say: "But offices were shut."
They say: "Not our clause. Not our concern."

HOW TO FIX IT:

Add working day logic:
"All references to 'day' shall mean working day unless otherwise specified."

Create holiday exception:
"Deadlines falling on official holidays or non-working days shall be deemed extended to the next working day."
Or build a hybrid:
"Where the period for performance or notice is seven days or fewer, 'days' shall mean working days."

Because sometimes, a Sunday is just a Sunday.

WTF SCORING SYSTEM™

Metric	Score
WTF Factor	9.3/10 – The Clause That Killed Christmas
Risk Profile	HIGH – Misses real-world logic, triggers artificial breaches
Verdict	REPLACE with 'working day' or ADD HOLIDAY tolerance clause

ENGINEERING TAKEAWAY:

If your contract counts every day, even when no one is working, you do not have a deadline.

You have a calendar ambush.

"A camel is a horse designed by a committee." – Issigonis

CLAUSE #35

"The Contractor Shall Ensure Compliance with all HSE Requirements of the Employer, Client, and Authority…"

aka: *The Clause That Blends Three Safety Systems into One Nightmare*

ENGINEER'S TRANSLATION:

"Follow our HSE plan. Also their HSE plan. Also the government's. Good luck when they contradict each other."

SATIRICAL INTERPRETATION:

This clause operates as a compliance blender, combining:

- The Employer's HSE specs
- The Engineer's safety policies
- Local Authority's legal mandates

Hit "Start," And what comes out?
A liability smoothie.

It is like being told:
"Drive at 60. Also drive at 40. And sometimes, stop entirely, depending on which sign is posted by whom."

You are now:

- Audited in three directions.
- Answerable to conflicting rules
- And blamed for failing to reconcile a contradiction nobody addressed.

WHY THIS IS A PROBLEM:

This clause creates a three-headed safety standard with one neck. You must comply with Employer, Client, and Authority HSE, simultaneously; even when they clash; even when no one agrees. It builds a compliance trap disguised as a duty of care. This clause shows up in:

- Preliminaries and General Requirements
- Safety plan appendices
- Local law compliance sections
- Prequalification and method statement approvals

It **sounds reasonable**, until:

- HSE spec A requires safety harnesses.
- Spec B prohibits working above 1.2m
- Authority C mandates a permit for both, issued monthly.

Now you are non-compliant no matter what you do.

LEGAL INSIGHT:

Multiple HSE regimes can coexist, but they must be organised. A contractor may be required to comply with statutory HSE law, Client requirements, and Employer procedures, but the contract should state which standard prevails where those requirements conflict, who decides the applicable rule, and whether compliance with a higher standard gives rise to time or cost relief.

In *MT Højgaard A/S v E.ON Climate & Renewables UK*[49] [2017] UKSC 59, the Supreme Court confirmed that overlapping technical requirements may be enforced where the contract clearly imposes a more rigorous obligation. Applied here, the danger is not safety. The danger is unmanaged hierarchy. If three HSE systems apply at once, the contract must identify priority, reconciliation procedure, and responsibility for resulting delay or cost.

WHERE THIS CREATES SAFETY MADNESS

You submit an HSE Plan aligned with the Employer's manual. The Client returns comments from their own plan (unshared until now). Meanwhile, the Municipality asks why your lifting plan was not signed in triplicate.

Now:

- You fail the audit.
- You stop work.
- You rewrite your HSE documents.
- You resubmit for approvals.

And all of it under Clause 5.7:
"The Contractor shall ensure compliance with all HSE requirements..."

HOW TO FIX IT:

Add hierarchy:

"Where multiple HSE requirements apply, precedence shall be as follows: Statutory Authority > Client > Employer."

Insert reconciliation clause:
"Where conflicting requirements arise, the Contractor shall notify the Employer, and the Employer shall determine the applicable standard."

---

49 MT Højgaard A/S v E.ON Climate & Renewables UK [2017] UKSC 59, United Kingdom (Supreme Court).

Limit ambiguity:
"Only formally issued and project-specific HSE requirements shall apply. General policy statements shall not override contractual documents."

Because no one can comply with three masters, especially when two are silent and one is changing the rules daily.

WTF SCORING SYSTEM™

Metric	Score
WTF Factor	9.1/10 – Safety By Committee (And Contradiction)
Risk Profile	HIGH – Failure by compliance overload
Verdict	CLARIFY PRECEDENCE or SPLIT INTO MULTIPLE, ALLOCATED CLAUSES

ENGINEERING TAKEAWAY:

You care about safety.
You want to comply.

But this clause guarantees that whatever you do, someone will say you did not do enough.

"All animals are equal, but some animals are more equal than others." – Orwell

CLAUSE #36

"The Contractor Acknowledges that Time is of the Essence, But this Shall not Be Construed as a Waiver of the Employer's Rights to Make Changes at Any Time."

aka: *The Clause That Respects Time, Until It's Their Turn*

ENGINEER'S TRANSLATION:

"You must be on time. We can take our time. And when our delays affect your timing, well, that is still on you."

SATIRICAL INTERPRETATION:

This clause loves punctuality, but only when it applies to you.

It says:
"Yes, time is of the essence. And yes, we might issue a variation mid-handover. Or submit a revised drawing 2 hours before commissioning. But the clock? Still ticking, on you."

It is the contractual equivalent of:
"We believe in accountability. Yours."

This clause treats "time" as a one-way street:

- Your delays = breach
- Their delays = flexibility
- Combined delays = your risk

WHY THIS IS A PROBLEM:

This clause says time is sacred, until the Employer is late. Then it is flexible; excusable; irrelevant. But when you are late, time becomes a breach. It is a stopwatch with a one-sided battery; a clock that only ticks in one direction, against you. This is a common two-faced clause found in:

- FIDIC Red Book Sub-Clause 8.1 hybrids
- EPC timing provisions
- Programme control and change order sections.
- Design & build contracts with variable scope.

It contradicts itself on purpose. It says:

"Time is sacred, except when we delay it."

And the problem is:

- No compensation
- No relief mechanism
- No suspension trigger

This clause is designed to preserve Employer power while demanding Contractor performance, in the same breath.

LEGAL INSIGHT:

In *Multiplex Construction (UK) Ltd v Honeywell Control Systems Ltd*[50] [2007] EWHC 447 (TCC), the court confirmed that Employer-caused delay does not automatically set time at large where the contract contains an operative EOT mechanism and the Contractor must use it. Clear notice and extension provisions can preserve the contractual completion regime.

In *Balfour Beatty Building Ltd v Chestermount Properties Ltd*[51] (1993) 62 BLR 1, the court considered how extension of time machinery operates where relevant events affect completion. Applied here, the risk is the one-sided combination: the Employer keeps its right to issue changes, while the Contractor remains bound to strict time obligations unless the clause expressly preserves reciprocal time relief. Time may be of the essence, but it should not be a one-way weapon.

WHERE THIS PLAYS OUT IN REAL LIFE

The Employer delays IFC drawings by 21 days. Meanwhile, you receive a variation instruction. But Clause 8.4 still says:

"Time remains of the essence. The Contractor shall mitigate delays without entitlement to cost or time unless approved."

You chase programme logic. They chase you for handover.

HOW TO FIX IT:

Add mutual time integrity:
"Time may be of the essence only where both Parties are bound by reciprocal time consequences. Delays by the Employer shall entitle the Contractor to time relief under Clause X.X."

---

50 Multiplex Construction (UK) Ltd v Honeywell Control Systems Ltd [2007] EWHC 447 (TCC), United Kingdom (Technology and Construction Court).

51 Balfour Beatty Building Ltd v Chestermount Properties Ltd (1993) 62 BLR 1, United Kingdom (Commercial Court).

Clarify variation impact:
"Variations issued after commencement shall include extension assessments as standard."

Respect causation:
"The Employer's right to make changes shall not operate to extinguish the Contractor's entitlement to time relief where such changes affect the critical path."

Because time cannot be essential only when it helps one side win the race.

WTF SCORING SYSTEM™

Metric	Score
WTF Factor	9.3/10 – Stopwatch With a One-Sided Timer
Risk Profile	HIGH – Double standard in delay responsibility
Verdict	MAKE TIME MUTUAL or LINK TO RELIEF MECHANISMS

ENGINEERING TAKEAWAY:

If time is truly of the essence, then everyone must honour the clock.

Otherwise, this clause is just a time bomb, with your name on it.

"Approval is temporary. Blame is forever."

– *Jinoy's Law on Construction Authority*

"Fools rush in where angels fear to tread." – Alexander Pope

CLAUSE #37

"The Contractor Shall Proceed with the Works at its Own Cost and Risk, Pending Formal Approval of the Variation…"

aka: *The Clause That Says, Trust Me, Bro'*

ENGINEER'S TRANSLATION:

"Do the extra work now. We will sort out the paperwork later. Maybe."

SATIRICAL INTERPRETATION:

This clause is pure optimism, weaponised.

It says:

"Go ahead. Mobilise. Weld. Pour. Procure. Do not worry, the variation will be formalised eventually. And if not, well, you took the risk."

You are now:

- Doing extra work
- Without price agreement
- Without time entitlement
- And somehow... without protection

This clause is the contractual equivalent of a blank cheque, where the cheque bounces, and you are blamed for accepting it.

WHY THIS IS A PROBLEM:

This clause turns initiative into exposure. It tells you to proceed with unpriced, unauthorised, undocumented work, based on a nod, a call, or a handshake. Then, when the bill comes due, it says: "No formal approval; no entitlement; no mercy." This is a notorious clause buried in:

- Variation clauses
- Instruction compliance sections
- Emergency or "urgent works" provisions
- Correspondence-based variation handling

It lures you with urgency. Then it removes your entitlement unless formally authorised, which often never comes.

LEGAL INSIGHT:

A Contractor who proceeds with changed or additional work before formal variation approval takes a serious entitlement risk. The safest route remains a written instruction, provisional valuation, express reservation of rights, and contemporaneous notice.

In *Molloy v Liebe*[52] (1910) 102 LT 616 (PC), the Employer refused to issue a formal instruction because it disputed whether the work was extra. The contractor carried out the work, and recovery was allowed when the work was later found to be outside the original scope. The case is useful, but dangerous

52 Molloy v Liebe (1910) 102 LT 616, Privy Council.

to rely on casually: it does not make verbal approval safe. It shows why disputed scope must be documented before proceeding, and why the contract should preserve payment where the Employer instructs, benefits from, or knowingly permits additional work.

WHERE THIS DEVOURS CONTRACTORS

You receive a verbal instruction:

"Shift the ducting by 1.5 metres. Just proceed, we will issue the VO later."

You proceed. Variation never issued. Six weeks later, your claim is rejected.

They quote Clause 13.3:
"Contractor proceeded at own cost and risk pending formal approval."
You went from proactive... to unpaid.

HOW TO FIX IT:

Require time-capped approval:

"The Contractor shall not be required to proceed with any varied or additional work unless a written instruction or provisional variation order is issued. Where the Employer instructs, permits, or knowingly benefits from changed work before formal approval, the Contractor's entitlement to time and cost shall be preserved, subject to timely notice and substantiation."

Proceeding under protest shall not prejudice the Contractor's entitlement, provided timely notice is served in accordance with Clause X.X.

Define binding thresholds:
"If works are performed in good faith on Employer instruction, payment shall not be denied solely due to procedural omission."

Add instruction protocol:
"No variation may proceed without at least provisional written instruction from the Engineer."

Because no one should do work based on hope and memory alone.

WTF SCORING SYSTEM™

Metric	Score
WTF Factor	9.4/10 – Verbal Promise, Written Denial
Risk Profile	CRITICAL – Work performed without guaranteed recovery
Verdict	REQUIRE WRITTEN INSTRUCTION or INSERT DEEMED APPROVAL MECHANISM

ENGINEERING TAKEAWAY:

Urgency is not entitlement.
Verbal instruction is not approval.

And this clause?
It turns initiative into liability.

Construction Lessons Series 017

"The first casualty of progress is the specification."

"Trust, but verify." – A Russian Proverb

CLAUSE #38

"The Contractor Confirms it has Independently Verified all Dimensions, Levels, and Site Conditions..."

aka: *The Clause That Makes You Responsible for the Laws of Physics*

ENGINEER'S TRANSLATION:

"If something is wrong, you, as an experienced Contractor should have seen it.
Even if it was underground.
Or on fire.
Or not yet built."

SATIRICAL INTERPRETATION:

This clause assumes you brought:

- A 4D scanner
- X-ray vision
- And divine insight
- A Crystal Ball
- A Ouija Board, all before you bid for the Project.

It says:
"You must verify all dimensions and site conditions before execution. So when you pour concrete off a drawing marked 'Preliminary,' and it goes wrong, guess what? Still your fault."

It is the ultimate 'you should have known' clause.
And if you did not?
Then you should have verified harder.

WHY THIS IS A PROBLEM:

This clause says you should know everything. The depths beneath the slab; the mislabeled drawings; the missing levels. It demands x-ray vision and hindsight as a skillset; then penalizes you for not verifying the future before it happened. You will see this clause in:

- Design & build tenders.
- Civil and structural works scopes
- Site access and mobilisation sections
- Subcontractor interface responsibilities

Its danger lies in:

- Transferring design/documentation defects to the Contractor
- Blocking claims for inaccurate or late data
- Suggesting site reality is yours to validate alone.

This clause makes you the official fact-checker of other people's mistakes.

LEGAL INSIGHT:

In *Tharsis Sulphur & Copper Co*[53] *v McElroy & Sons* (1878) 3 App Cas 1040, the House of Lords held that a contractor who had undertaken to satisfy itself whether the specified work could be done could not recover additional cost

53 Tharsis Sulphur & Copper Co v McElroy & Sons (1878) 3 App Cas 1040, United Kingdom (House of Lords).

merely because the work proved more difficult than expected. The risk had been accepted under the contract unless a valid written instruction changed it.

Applied here, the danger is the breadth of "independently verified". Verification should be limited to matters reasonably accessible, visible, measurable, and capable of verification before execution. It should not make the Contractor responsible for hidden conditions, inaccurate Employer data, latent dimensional conflicts, undisclosed utilities, or information that only becomes available after the contract is signed.

WHERE THIS SHIFTS FAULT

You construct a base slab per the issued IFC (Issued for Construction Drawings).
Two months later, a steel structure subbie says:
"Your level is 110mm off."

You say: "I used the IFC dimensions."
They say:
"Clause 2.2: Contractor must verify all dimensions independently."

You point to the topographical survey.
They point to the clause again.
And suddenly, the drawing's wrong, but the liability is yours.

HOW TO FIX IT:

Qualify verification:
"Verification shall be limited to conditions, dimensions, and levels that were reasonably accessible, visible, measurable, and capable of verification at the time of inspection."

Add information accuracy clause:
"The Contractor shall be entitled to rely on design and reference documents issued by the Employer unless expressly notified of error."

Insert shared risk provision:
"Errors resulting from inaccurate Employer data shall be treated as compensable variations under Clause X.X."

Because you cannot be expected to verify what you cannot see, control, or influence.

WTF SCORING SYSTEM™

Metric	Score
WTF Factor	9.3/10 – Fault Finding by Retrospective ESP
Risk Profile	HIGH – Transforms design flaws into Contractor fault
Verdict	QUALIFY scope of verification or SHIFT BACK DESIGN LIABILITY where applicable

ENGINEERING TAKEAWAY:

You can check levels.
You can verify site access.
But when the clause says you must verify everything, it is quietly assigning you responsibility for everyone else's errors.

"Forgive your enemies—but never forget their invoice." – Jinoy's unwritten Law

CLAUSE #39

"Any Failure or Delay By the Employer to Exercise its Rights Shall not Be Deemed a Waiver..."

aka: *The Clause That Remembers Everything You Forgot*

ENGINEER'S TRANSLATION:

"If you miss a deadline, you are in breach.

If we miss it, we reserve the right to remember it later and penalise you retroactively."

SATIRICAL INTERPRETATION:

This clause is the Employer's amnesia insurance policy.
It says:
"Just because we did not enforce our rights yesterday... does not mean we will not next month. Or next year. Or at final account."

Imagine a referee who:

- Watches the foul.
- Says nothing.
- Waits until halftime.
- Then ejects you from the game.

That is this clause.
It does not forgive, it delays vengeance.

WHY THIS IS A PROBLEM:

This clause forgives nothing. It watches you fail silently; it lets you believe the breach was waived; then resurrects the issue when it matters most, at final account. It gives the Employer a memory that only activates when you have something to lose. This clause lurks in:

- Default and breach sections.
- LD and claim enforcement clauses.
- Contract interpretation appendices.
- Boilerplate dispute provisions

It lets the Employer:

- Delay action
- Stay silent.
- Then **resurrect penalties** as if they were never waived.

LEGAL INSIGHT:

A non-waiver clause can preserve contractual rights even where a party delays enforcement or remains silent for a period. But it is not absolute. If the other party has relied on that silence, continued performance, or repeated inaction to its detriment, waiver, estoppel, or election arguments may still arise depending on the wording, conduct, and governing law.

The danger is timing. The Employer may say silence was only reservation, while the Contractor says silence was acceptance. Without a notice period, reservation requirement, or reliance carve-out, this clause turns inaction into a weapon and makes the Contractor prove that quiet conduct had legal consequences.

WHERE THIS CAUSES REPUTATIONAL WHIPLASH

You submit monthly reports 2 days late for 4 months.
Nothing happens.
No notices. No warnings.
At final account:

"Clause 17.6: You consistently failed to submit reports on time. This supports our application of LDs in full."

You say: "But you never objected."
They say: "Clause 21.9, our silence was not a waiver."

And now you are being penalised for something you thought was forgiven or forgotten.

HOW TO FIX IT:

Add a notification clause:
"Where the Employer fails to act within 21 days, the right shall be deemed waived for that event unless otherwise notified."

Limit retroactivity:
"Rights not exercised within 60 days of the event shall be time-barred unless otherwise agreed in writing."

Introduce fairness:
"No failure or delay shall constitute waiver, provided that the right is exercised within a reasonable time and before the Contractor has relied upon such inaction to its detriment."

Because no one should be punished for assuming silence meant acceptance, especially when the other party said nothing. For months.

WTF SCORING SYSTEM™

Metric	Score
WTF Factor	9.3/10 – Silent Now, Savage Later
Risk Profile	HIGH – Retroactive penalty trap
Verdict	ADD TIMELINE FOR ENFORCEMENT or REMOVE SWEEPING NON-WAIVER CLAUSE

ENGINEERING TAKEAWAY:

If your contract says their silence is never a waiver, then you are playing a game where only one side gets to use the clock.

"Approval is temporary; blame is permanent." – Jinoy's unwritten Law

CLAUSE #40

"The Employer's Approval Shall not Relieve the Contractor of Any Liability..."

aka: *The Clause That Approves You, Then Abandons You*

ENGINEER'S TRANSLATION:

"We approved your work.
We used your work.
But if anything goes wrong, we never saw it."

SATIRICAL INTERPRETATION:

This clause says:
"We reviewed your design, stamped it, commented on it, and approved it. But just to be clear, we are not responsible for any of that. You are."

It is the contractual version of:
"You are free to make your own decisions. As long as we approve them. And you take the blame."

If the Employer reviews, interferes, delays, or even redesigns it, you are still liable.

Because approval is just… a suggestion.

WHY THIS IS A PROBLEM:

This clause approves your work and then walks away. It stamps your design; nods at your submittal; accepts your method; then tells you the consequences are still yours. It turns review into rejection and approval into abandonment. This clause appears in:

- Design & build contracts.
- Shop drawing and material submittal clauses.
- Method statement approvals
- Commissioning and test plan reviews

It neutralises the entire review process.

This clause formalises that rule, giving the Employer the right to review and comment without necessarily assuming responsibility.

LEGAL INSIGHT:

Approval does not automatically transfer liability. Where the contract states that Employer or Engineer approval does not relieve the Contractor, the Contractor may remain responsible even after review, comment, stamping, or acceptance of the submission. See also MT Hojgaard A/S v E.ON Climate & Renewables UK Ltd.[54]

The danger lies in unqualified approval language. If the Employer's review merely checks compliance, the Contractor may still carry the risk. But where the Employer's approval, comment, or instruction materially changes the design basis, restricts compliant alternatives, or causes the Contractor reasonably to rely on a directed solution, the contract should preserve a corresponding adjustment of responsibility. Otherwise, approval becomes a one-way safeguard: the Employer controls the process, while the Contractor owns the consequence.

---

54 MT Højgaard A/S v E.ON Climate & Renewables UK Ltd [2017] UKSC 59, United Kingdom (Supreme Court).

WHERE THIS UNDERMINES REASONABLE RELIANCE

You submit a design detail for review.
Engineer says: *"Approved with comments."*
You proceed. The detail fails in inspection.

The Employer says:
*"We approved it. But Clause 14.5 means that does not matter.
You are still fully responsible."*

So their approval? Not worth the PDF it was stamped on.

HOW TO FIX IT:

Add shared responsibility:
"Where the Employer's approval, instruction, or review comments materially influence the adopted design or method, liability shall be shared proportionally."

Clarify intent:
"Approval shall not relieve the Contractor of liability except where the Contractor has reasonably relied upon Employer approval or instruction in circumstances where alternative compliance was no longer practicable."

Require escalation:
"Disputed design rejections must be escalated under Clause X.X to avoid unilateral risk assignment."

Otherwise, the clause gives them editorial rights without editorial responsibility.

WTF SCORING SYSTEM™

Metric	Score
WTF Factor	9.2/10 – Stamped, Approved, Still Screwed
Risk Profile	HIGH – Review becomes trap instead of safeguard
Verdict	INSERT SHARED RISK or REWRITE to limit unqualified approval language

ENGINEERING TAKEAWAY:

If they review your work…
If they approve your work…

But still disown the result,
Then you are not working with an approver.
You are collaborating with a silent witness.

"If you can't build it without drawings, build it anyway—the drawings will arrive just in time to prove you wrong."

– Jinoy's Law on Construction Execution

"Even blind faith needs a plan." – Jinoy's unwritten Law

CLAUSE #41

"The Contractor Shall Maintain Full Progress Notwithstanding Delay in Receiving Drawings, Information, or Instructions..."

aka: *The Clause That Thinks You Can Build Without Data*

ENGINEER'S TRANSLATION:

"Even if we delay issuing the drawings, you must not delay the work. Keep going. Invent if you have to."

SATIRICAL INTERPRETATION:

This clause imagines your site runs on:

- Faith
- Intuition
- And a Ouija board

It says:
"You must maintain progress, even if the drawings, specs, and instructions arrive late. Or never."

In other words:

- Design is optional.
- Scope is flexible.
- Liability? Still yours

This is not project management. It is project clairvoyance.

WHY THIS IS A PROBLEM:

This clause demands performance without information; it expects the Contractor to maintain full progress, even when the Employer withholds the very documents required to proceed. It turns delay in deliverables into Contractor fault. If progress obligations are unconditional, risk passes fully to the Contractor, even when performance becomes impractical. Even when critical data is missing, this clause demands uninterrupted progress, converting lack of information into Contractor liability without relief or logic.

This clause shows up in:

- Programme and scheduling provisions.
- Contractor obligations under Clause 8 (FIDIC derivatives)
- Interim design-build frameworks
- Subcontract general obligations.

Its impact:

- Contractor is forced to progress blind.
- Employer holds back critical information.
- Yet still enforces programme and LDs.

This clause says so. Explicitly.

LEGAL INSIGHT:

A progress obligation can be enforced where the Contractor has the information, access, and instructions needed to perform. The danger begins when the clause demands full progress while the Employer withholds, delays, or fails to issue the very documents required for performance.

This is not ordinary programme discipline. It is risk transfer by fiction. If drawings, information, approvals, or instructions are Employer deliverables, the contract should link progress obligations to their timely release. Without that link, the Contractor may be blamed for delay caused by missing data, while still being required to maintain a programme built on assumptions.

WHERE THIS RUINS LOGIC ON SITE

You wait for IFC drawings for the control room. They are delayed 21 days. Meanwhile, your progress report is flagged.

The Engineer says:
"Clause 8.5: Full progress must be maintained, even if drawings are delayed."

You say: "I cannot fabricate steel off blank paper."

They say: "That's a planning issue."
Now your critical path delay is your responsibility because you refused to build a control room with no controls.

HOW TO FIX IT:

Make progress conditional:
"The Contractor shall maintain progress only where drawings, information, and instructions are provided in accordance with the agreed schedule. Where the Contractor proceeds to mitigate notwithstanding missing information, such mitigation shall not be construed as acceptance of risk or waiver of entitlement."

Link to Extension of Time (EOT) entitlement:
"Any delay in receiving Employer deliverables shall entitle the Contractor to programme adjustment and cost/time relief."

Protect programme integrity:
"Unavailability of design shall be treated as an Employer delay under Clause X.X and reflected in Window Analysis entitlement."

Because progress without information is just motion, not performance.

WTF SCORING SYSTEM™

Metric	Score
WTF Factor	9.4/10 – Deliverables Optional, Deadlines Mandatory
Risk Profile	CRITICAL – Shifts all delay risk to Contractor regardless of data flow
Verdict	LINK TO TIMELY INFORMATION or QUALIFY "FULL PROGRESS" TO REAL CONDITIONS

ENGINEERING TAKEAWAY:

A project needs drawings. Instructions. Clarity. But this clause?

They give you 30% drawings, a missing Issued for Construction Drawings (IFC) package, and a half-nod on Teams, then wonder why your progress report shows zero. This clause? It does not care. It wants you to mobilise anyway.

"Rules for thee, but not for me." – Aphorism

CLAUSE #42

"The Contractor Shall not Assign or Subcontract the Works without Employer's Consent. The Employer May Assign Freely."

***aka:** The Clause That Says, 'One Rule for You, None for Me'*

ENGINEER'S TRANSLATION:

"If you want to change anything, ask us. If we want to change everything, you will find out in a circular."

SATIRICAL INTERPRETATION:

This clause has two faces and one beneficiary. It says:

"You must seek approval for any assignment, subcontract, or team change. We can hand the entire contract to another entity, without telling you until it is done."

You are required to:

- Get consent before shifting your site engineer.
- But they can replace the Employer with a holding company in the Cayman Islands and call it continuity.

It is the legal equivalent of:

"You may not move. We may vanish and reappear wearing someone else's logo."

WHY THIS IS A PROBLEM:

This clause institutionalizes asymmetry, restricting the Contractor's movement while granting the Employer unchecked freedom to reassign the entire contract without consequence. This clause enforces a double standard in legal mobility; the Contractor must seek approval for every change, while the Employer can replace itself entirely, without notice, negotiation, or consequence.

You will see this clause in:

- Assignment and novation sections
- Subcontracting provisions
- Owner-Contractor obligation clauses
- Termination and transfer structures

The risks?

- Employer assigns to SPVs with no assets
- You lose enforcement power.
- You inherit a new counterparty you did not choose.
- All without negotiation or recourse

This clause gives them the same freedom, without extending it to you.

LEGAL INSIGHT:

Assignment rights are governed by the contract. In *Linden Gardens Trust Ltd v Lenesta Sludge Disposals Ltd*[55] [1994] 1 AC 85, the House of Lords confirmed

55 Linden Gardens Trust Ltd v Lenesta Sludge Disposals Ltd [1994] 1 AC 85, United Kingdom (House of Lords).

that contractual restrictions on assignment can be effective where clearly drafted. The principle cuts both ways: if the contract restricts the Contractor but permits the Employer to assign freely, courts will usually begin with that bargain.

The danger is asymmetry. The Contractor may be locked into performance, consent requirements, and approval procedures, while the Employer can transfer contractual rights to a new entity with different financial standing, decision-makers, or enforcement profile. Assignment may be legally permitted, but without safeguards it can materially alter the commercial risk of the project.

WHERE THIS FLIPS THE TABLE ON YOU

You request to subcontract façade works to a certified vendor.
It takes three weeks, three reminders, and six revised method statements to get approval.

Meanwhile, you receive a letter:
"Please note that effective today, the Employer has assigned all rights to XYZ Holdings Limited."

No negotiation.
No risk analysis.
Just a new party, and a new layer of confusion.

HOW TO FIX IT:

Demand mutuality:
"Neither Party shall assign or subcontract its obligations without the written consent of the other."
Add constraint language:
"Assignment by either Party shall not adversely affect accrued rights, payment security, governing law, dispute forum, approval history, or existing project commitments."

Insert Contractor's right of refusal:
"Where the Employer assigns the Contract to a financially weaker or offshore entity, the Contractor shall have the right to suspend performance pending reassessment."

Because if you are expected to get permission for minor changes, they should not be allowed to rewrite the counterparty overnight.

WTF SCORING SYSTEM™

Metric	Score
WTF Factor	9.2/10 – Contractual Double Standard
Risk Profile	HIGH – Loss of control over legal counterparty
Verdict	ENFORCE reciprocity or ADD CONTRACTOR'S RIGHT to object to assignment

ENGINEERING TAKEAWAY:

If you need consent to hire a subcontractor, but they can change who pays you, owns you, and sues you, then you are not in a contract.

You are in a corporate power play.

"Any fool can make a rule, and every fool will mind it." – Thoreau

CLAUSE #43

"In the Event of Conflict, the More Stringent Requirement Shall Prevail..."

***aka:** The Clause That Automatically Picks the Hardest Option*

ENGINEER'S TRANSLATION:

"If two clauses contradict each other, pick the one that hurts you most. That is what we meant."

SATIRICAL INTERPRETATION:

This clause is not here to clarify. It is here to intensify.

It says:
"If the contract confuses you, pick the version with the tighter deadline, stricter penalty, or higher cost. That one is correct."

Imagine a riddle where every wrong answer is punishable, and the hardest option is always right by default.

It is like asking which fire exit to use in an emergency,
and being told:
"Take the one with more flames. It must be safer; it is more stringent."

WHY THIS IS A PROBLEM:

This clause replaces clarity with cruelty; it instructs that when two provisions conflict, the harsher one must win, even if it was unintended, unfeasible, or commercially absurd. Rather than resolving ambiguity through fairness or intent, this clause imposes the harshest default, no matter how impractical or commercially unreasonable.

You will find this clause in:

- Technical compliance sections
- Contract interpretation appendices.
- Specification-document conflict clauses
- Design-build hybrids and multi-authority projects.

Its effect:

- Ambiguity is not resolved by logic.
- It is resolved by choosing the harshest interpretation.
- Even if that contradicts common sense, fairness, or programme feasibility.

LEGAL INSIGHT:

In *MT Højgaard A/S v E.ON Climate & Renewables UK*[56] [2017] UKSC 59, the Supreme Court confirmed that where a contract contains overlapping technical standards, a more demanding obligation may be enforceable if the contract clearly imposes it. Compliance with one standard may not be enough if another part of the contract requires a higher performance outcome.

This is the same trap seen in Clauses #25, #35, and #40: the Contractor complies with one standard, receives review or approval, and still loses because another clause quietly imposes the harder obligation.

Applied here, the danger is automatic severity. "More stringent shall prevail" may be workable where the conflicting requirements are clearly identified

56 MT Højgaard A/S v E.ON Climate & Renewables UK [2017] UKSC 59, United Kingdom (Supreme Court).

and technically compatible. But if the clause is used as a universal shortcut, it can convert drafting inconsistency into extra cost, programme pressure, and rework. The safer answer is a defined order of precedence, reasoned clarification, and a requirement that the stricter option must be technically necessary, buildable, and priced.

WHERE THIS HIJACKS CONTRACT INTERPRETATION

Specification A says concrete strength shall be 40 MPa.
Specification B says 45 MPa.

You raise an Request for Information (RFI).

No reply.
You build to 40 MPa.

Engineer says:
"Clause 1.6: Where conflict exists, the more stringent requirement shall apply. You are non-compliant."

Now you owe rework, for following the design that made more sense.

HOW TO FIX IT:

Insert precedence logic:
"In the event of conflict, documents shall be interpreted in accordance with the order of precedence listed in Appendix Y."

Require reasoned resolution:

"No stricter requirement shall apply unless it is technically necessary, commercially priced, and capable of compliance within the agreed programme."

Delete extremity logic:

"The more stringent requirement shall not apply where it contradicts the agreed programme, pricing, or design parameters."

Because ambiguity should be resolved by intention, not punishment.

WTF SCORING SYSTEM™

Metric	Score
WTF Factor	9.3/10 – Choose Your Own Punishment
Risk Profile	HIGH – Turns ambiguity into automatic hardship
Verdict	USE DOCUMENT PRECEDENCE or REQUIRE CLARIFICATION BEFORE ENFORCEMENT

ENGINEERING TAKEAWAY:

When two requirements conflict, the correct response is not "do both." It is "ask for clarity."

But this clause says: "Make it harder and make it your fault."

"To err is human; to blame it on the contractor is project management." – Parody

CLAUSE #44

"The Contractor Shall Ensure that no Claims Arise Due to Errors or Discrepancies in the Contract Documents..."

***aka:** The Clause That Blames You for Their Typos*

ENGINEER'S TRANSLATION:

"If our drawings contradict our specs, and that causes a delay, you are not allowed to claim. Because you should have caught it."

SATIRICAL INTERPRETATION:

This clause does not just shift risk.
It shifts authorship.

It says:
"The Employer prepared the contract. But if we made mistakes, those are your fault now. Thanks for spotting them (eventually)."

This is not just unreasonable. It is reverse authorship by liability.

You did not write the documents. You did not design the works. But you are expected to:

- Detect every contradiction.
- Fix it without delay.
- And definitely not raise a claim

It is the contract version of:
"Please mind our errors, quietly."

WHY THIS IS A PROBLEM:

This clause shifts the blame for contradictions, the Contractor did not write; it punishes the Contractor for not discovering discrepancies in the Employer's own documents and turns their drafting failure into your liability. By shifting responsibility for contradictions or defects in the Employer's own documents, this clause turns due diligence into an unreasonable burden and neutralizes legitimate claims.

You will find this clause in:

- FIDIC Red/Yellow hybrid amendments
- Subcontractor scope qualification disclaimers
- General obligation sections
- Drafted Employer-side bespoke documents

Its real agenda:

- Block disruption claims.
- Disqualify claims based on confusion or ambiguity.
- Create Contractor liability for someone else's drafting error.

This clause says otherwise.

LEGAL INSIGHT:

A Contractor can be required to review the contract documents and notify discrepancies. That is not the same as accepting authorship of those documents. Where the Employer prepares or issues drawings, specifications, schedules, or tender clarifications, the contract should distinguish between a duty to identify apparent inconsistencies and liability for errors the Contractor did not create.

The danger lies in turning review into warranty. If the clause makes the Contractor responsible for all consequences of Employer document errors, it converts coordination into authorship and due diligence into blame. A fair clause should limit the Contractor's responsibility to discrepancies reasonably detectable before execution and preserve entitlement where the error arises from Employer-issued information, late clarification, or conflicting contractual documents.

WHERE THIS KILLS YOUR CLAIM

You proceed based on the IFC drawings.
The specifications contradict them.
Your materials are rejected.
The rework delays the critical path.
You raise a claim.

They say:
"Clause 4.11: You shall ensure no claims arise due to discrepancies in our documents."

You say: "But you created the conflict."

They say: "And you accepted it."
Now the clause that should have protected you… has accused you.

HOW TO FIX IT:

Assign liability where it belongs:
"The Employer shall remain responsible for discrepancies, conflicts, or omissions in documents prepared, issued, or approved by the Employer, except to the extent such discrepancies were reasonably apparent and not notified by the Contractor before execution."

Permit claims:
"Nothing in this clause shall prevent the Contractor from raising claims arising from ambiguity or conflict between Employer-issued documents."

Introduce reasonable expectation:
"The Contractor shall not be held liable for discrepancies not reasonably detectable during tender or execution."

Because error detection is not error creation, and this clause forgets that entirely.

WTF SCORING SYSTEM™

Metric	Score
WTF Factor	9.3/10 – Drafted by You, Billed to Me
Risk Profile	HIGH – Denies recovery for document-driven delay
Verdict	LIMIT to reasonable detection or REASSIGN LIABILITY for employer's errors

ENGINEERING TAKEAWAY:

You did not draft the documents.
You did not contradict the drawings.

But this clause insists you spotted them… and still denies your claim.

"To err is human; to blame it on someone else shows management potential."
– Anonymous

CLAUSE #45

"The Contractor Shall Indemnify the Employer Against All Claims Arising From the Use of Any Design Provided By the Employer…"

***aka:** The Clause That Gives You a Broken Map, Then Charges You for Getting Lost*

ENGINEER'S TRANSLATION:

"Use our design. But if it causes a problem, we will blame you for following it."

SATIRICAL INTERPRETATION:

This clause is an Employer-issued trap, wrapped in CAD (Computer aided design) lines and sealed with indemnity.

It says:
"We gave you the design. You had no authority to change it. But if anything goes wrong, we will say you should have known better."

It is the legal version of:
"Here is the GPS route. Please follow it. If you drive off a cliff, we will invoice you."

You are:

- Given an approved drawing
- Forbidden from deviating.
- Then blamed for the consequences of obedience.

WHY THIS IS A PROBLEM:

This clause removes all protection for following instructions; it makes the Contractor responsible for defects in Employer-issued design, even when you are not allowed to change a single line. This clause imposes liability for faithfully executing Employer-supplied design, converting obedience into fault, and erasing the Employer's design accountability.

You will find this clause in:

- D&C hybrid contracts
- Employer-designed scope sections
- EPC contracts with retained design authority
- Subcontractor agreements in turnkey projects

Its purpose?

To convert design followership into design liability, without recourse.

This clause removes that exclusion, and places you squarely in the firing line.

LEGAL INSIGHT:

In *Plant Construction plc v Clive Adams Associates*[57] [2000] EWHC Technology 119, the court confirmed that a contractor may still be liable where it follows an Employer's or Engineer's unsafe instruction but fails to give an adequate warning, or fails to refuse to proceed where the danger is obvious.

57 Plant Construction plc v Clive Adams Associates [2000] EWHC Technology 119, United Kingdom (Technology and Construction Court).

Applied here, the danger is the reverse burden. The Contractor should not become the insurer of every Employer-provided design merely because it used it. Liability should depend on control, authority to change, knowledge of defect, and whether the Contractor knew or ought reasonably to have known that the design was unsafe, defective, or unbuildable. Indemnity for Employer design should therefore be tied to the Contractor's negligence, failure to warn, unauthorised deviation, or breach, not mere obedience.

WHERE THIS TRIPS YOU INTO LIABILITY

You follow the Employer's design for a pipe rack.
The layout causes vibration issues.
The Client raises a claim. The Employer forwards it to you.
You say: "I followed your IFC drawings."

They say:

"Clause 5.9: Contractor shall indemnify the Employer against all claims arising from use of Employer-provided design."

So you did exactly what they told you to, and now you are paying for the consequences.

HOW TO FIX IT:

Limit indemnity:

"The Contractor shall not indemnify the Employer for defects in Employer-provided design except to the extent caused by the Contractor's unauthorised deviation, negligent modification, failure to warn of an obvious defect, or breach of an express review obligation."

Add review rights:

"Design issued by Employer shall be subject to Contractor's review, and any defects discovered shall be notified, not indemnified."

Reassign source-based liability:

"Responsibility for Employer design errors shall remain with the Employer unless the Contractor knew, or ought reasonably to have known, of an obvious defect and failed to notify it."

Because no one should be punished for trusting the map they were ordered to follow. This does not exclude Contractor liability where the Contractor has design discretion, review responsibility, or authority to modify the Employer's design.

WTF SCORING SYSTEM™

Metric	Score
WTF Factor	9.4/10 – Blamed for Blind Obedience
Risk Profile	CRITICAL – Turns following instructions into fault
Verdict	REMOVE OR REVERSE LIABILITY or TIE INDEMNITY to design control & review rights

ENGINEERING TAKEAWAY:

You followed the design.

You followed the instruction.

But the clause says you should have known better. Even when "better" was not in your control.

"Experience is what you get when the Employer forgets the lesson."

– Jinoy's Final Construction law

"Assumption is the mother of all mistakes." – Military Proverb

CLAUSE #46

"The Contractor is Deemed to Have Fully Understood the Employer's Requirements, Even Where Not Expressly Stated."

aka: *The Clause That Reads Minds*

ENGINEER'S TRANSLATION:

"We will not write it down.
We will not explain it.
But you are still expected to get it right."

SATIRICAL INTERPRETATION:

This clause gives you a scope of work, strips out 20% of the detail, adds 10% hidden assumptions, and says:

"You are deemed to have understood the full intention of the Employer, whether or not we expressed it."

You are now liable for:

- Unstated expectations
- Future clarifications
- Implied logic
- And any "common sense" they think you should have applied ...in hindsight.

This clause turns contract comprehension into clairvoyance.

WHY THIS IS A PROBLEM:

This clause demands clairvoyance; it holds the Contractor liable for unwritten expectations and undocumented intent, converting silence into scope and assumption into obligation. This clause expects the Contractor to meet undocumented intentions and implied expectations, creating liability for what was never written, never clarified, and never agreed.

You will find this clause in:

- Design & Build Employer's Requirements disclaimers.
- EPC tenders with rushed Employer's Requirements
- Vague Employer Requirement documents
- Poorly defined functional performance specs

Its aim?

- Block scope variation claims.
- Deny design clarifications.
- Hold you liable for mismatches between what they meant and what they wrote.

LEGAL INSIGHT:

In *RSP Architects Planners & Engineers v Mott MacDonald Singapore*[58] [2014] SGHC 72, the court examined whether additional payment could be claimed outside a lump-sum contractual framework. The case is useful because it

58 RSP Architects Planners & Engineers v Mott MacDonald Singapore Pte Ltd [2014] SGHC 72, Singapore (High Court).

shows that scope is assessed from the contract, its context, and objectively ascertainable requirements, not from a party's later assertion of what it meant.

Applied here, the danger is the word "deemed". A contractor may be held to what the contract objectively required, but that is different from being made liable for unstated expectations, hidden intent, or requirements never expressed in the documents. If the Employer wants a performance requirement, it should be written, ranked, and priced. Otherwise, the clause turns interpretation into mind-reading.

WHERE THIS SABOTAGES YOUR ENTITLEMENT

The Employer wants acoustic insulation.
It is not in the BOQ.
Not in the drawings.
Not in the spec.
You build what was documented. Later, they say:

"You are deemed to have understood our full performance intent."

You say: "It was never stated."
They say: "Clause 3.2, 'expressly or otherwise.' You should have inferred it."
You are now in breach for following what was written, not what was imagined.

HOW TO FIX IT:

Kill the ambiguity:
"The Contractor's obligations are limited to requirements expressly stated in, or objectively ascertainable from, the Contract Documents, drawings, specifications, and formally issued clarifications."

Permit clarification:
"Where Employer requirements are ambiguous or incomplete, Contractor shall seek written clarification and proceed accordingly."

Reject retrospective logic:
"The Contractor shall not be liable for unstated requirements or interpretation gaps in Employer-issued documents unless such requirements were clearly identifiable from the Contract Documents and reasonably capable of being priced at tender."

Because if they wanted something done, they should have written it down.

WTF SCORING SYSTEM™

Metric	Score
WTF Factor	9.6/10 – Mind Reading Clause
Risk Profile	CRITICAL – Punishes based on assumptions, not documentation
Verdict	REMOVE "IMPLIED" wording or LIMIT LIABILITY to stated scope only

ENGINEERING TAKEAWAY:

If a clause says you are "deemed to have understood" the Employer's requirements, then you are not being asked to build.

You are being asked to divine.

"He who writes the rules wins the game." – Proverb

CLAUSE #47

"Any Ambiguities Shall Be Interpreted in Favour of the Employer."

aka: *The Clause That Gives You the Paper, and Takes the Pen*

ENGINEER'S TRANSLATION:

"If something in the contract is unclear, we will decide what it means. And you will accept it."

SATIRICAL INTERPRETATION:

This clause says:
"The contract is ours. The ambiguity is yours. The interpretation? Still ours."

It is the legal equivalent of:
"Heads we win, tails you misunderstood the clause."

You are now signing a document that:

- Allows one party to create the confusion.
- And gives that same party exclusive interpretive power.
- Even in disputes that arise from their own drafting.

It is not just one-sided. It is the referee playing for the other team.

WHY THIS IS A PROBLEM:

This clause attempts to remove neutrality from interpretation by allocating ambiguity to the Employer, giving the drafting party both control over the language and an asserted right to determine its meaning, subject to judicial scrutiny.

Instead of upholding neutral interpretation, this clause shifts all doubt to the Contractor's detriment, even when the ambiguity stems from Employer-authored contradictions.

This clause appears in:

- Dispute resolution and interpretation appendices.
- Final pages of Employer-issued bespoke contracts
- Government tender forms with layered documentation

Its job is to:

- Override *contra proferentem* (interpret against the drafter)
- Tip every interpretive question in the Employer's favour.
- Deflect ambiguity blame, even when the Employer caused the ambiguity.

LEGAL INSIGHT:

Ambiguity is not normally resolved by giving one party permanent control over meaning. Courts first construe the contract as a whole, applying the words used, the commercial context, and the objective purpose of the agreement.

In *Canada Steamship Lines Ltd*[59] *v The King* [1952] AC 192, the Privy Council treated ambiguous exclusion wording cautiously, particularly where one party sought to avoid liability. In *Persimmon Homes Ltd*[60] *v Ove Arup & Partners Ltd* [2017] EWCA Civ 373, the Court of Appeal confirmed the modern position: in negotiated commercial contracts, contra proferentem has a limited role where the language is clear. Applied here, a clause that gives every ambiguity to the

---

59 Canada Steamship Lines Ltd v The King [1952] AC 192, United Kingdom (Privy Council).

60 Persimmon Homes Ltd v Ove Arup & Partners Ltd [2017] EWCA Civ 373, United Kingdom (Court of Appeal).

Employer may be effective if clear, but it is still a warning sign: the drafter is trying to control both the confusion and the answer.

WHERE THIS REWRITES THE RULES, AFTER KICKOFF

The contract drawings show 1200mm duct risers.
The specification calls for 900mm.
The BOQ says 1000mm.

You query. No response.

At variation time, the Employer says:
"Clause 1.9: Any ambiguity shall be interpreted in favour of the Employer. 900mm it is. Your price is nonconforming."

Now you owe them money, for their own contradiction.

HOW TO FIX IT:

Restore balance:
"In the event of ambiguity, interpretation shall favour the party not responsible for drafting the provision in question."

Enforce clarification duty:
"Ambiguities shall be raised within 14 days of discovery and resolved jointly in writing."

Add dispute fallback:
"Ambiguous clauses shall be interpreted in accordance with the commercial purpose of the Contract."

Because you cannot allow one party to both confuse the language and then interpret it unilaterally.

WTF SCORING SYSTEM™

Metric	Score
WTF Factor	9.5/10 – Drafted by You, Decided by You
Risk Profile	CRITICAL – Removes neutral dispute interpretation
Verdict	DELETE OR NEUTRALISE or REPLACE with bilateral interpretation rule

ENGINEERING TAKEAWAY:

If they draft the contract, cause the ambiguity, and then legally control the meaning, you are not negotiating.

You are signing a confession.

"If you want something blamed, give it to the contractor." – Parody

CLAUSE #48

"The Contractor Shall Be Responsible for the Acts and Omissions of the Employer's Nominated Subcontractors."

aka: *The Clause That Blames You for People You Cannot Control*

ENGINEER'S TRANSLATION:

"We chose them.
We told you to use them.
They delayed you.
And now it is your problem."

SATIRICAL INTERPRETATION:

This clause is a liability trap in subcontractor clothing.
It says:
"You are fully responsible for the subcontractor you did not select, cannot replace, and are not allowed to direct."

You become:

- The scapegoat for delays
- The absorber of rework
- The unpaid babysitter for a third party

It is the contractual version of:
"Here, hold this grenade. No, you cannot let go. Yes, it is already live."

WHY THIS IS A PROBLEM:

This clause transfers risk without authority; it makes the Contractor liable for the acts of nominated parties over whom they have no control, effectively punishing you for someone else's appointment. It allocates full responsibility to the Contractor for third parties they did not select, cannot instruct, and are barred from replacing, erasing the very concept of control-based liability.

This clause is often hidden in:

- Subcontractor coordination provisions
- Employer-nominated vendor frameworks (FIDIC Sub-Clause 5.1)
- Government or client-imposed sourcing obligations
- Public works tenders where vendor pools are pre-locked.

Its effect:

- You carry full risk for parties outside your contract chain.
- You cannot enforce timelines or quality.
- But you absorb the impact of both.

Unless the Contractor is granted meaningful control, contractual authority, payment levers, and programming access, liability cannot fairly attach. This clause tries to make that control irrelevant.

LEGAL INSIGHT:

In *Percy Bilton Ltd v Greater London Council*[61] [1982] 1 WLR 794, the House of Lords treated nominated subcontractor failure according to the contract's risk

---

61 Percy Bilton Ltd v Greater London Council [1982] 1 WLR 794, United Kingdom (House of Lords).

allocation. The withdrawal or default of a nominated subcontractor did not automatically give the main contractor an extension of time unless the contract provided a route to relief.

Applied here, the danger is clear. If the Contractor is made responsible for nominated subcontractors, the clause must also give the Contractor meaningful control: objection rights, programme access, coordination authority, replacement rights, payment leverage, and relief where the nominated party delays or defaults outside the Contractor's control. Otherwise, responsibility follows nomination, but control does not.

WHERE THIS WRECKS YOUR EOT

The Employer nominates a specialist BMS (Building Management System) contractor.
They delay by 6 weeks. You raise an EOT claim.

They respond:
"Clause 7.8: Contractor is responsible for acts and omissions of nominated subcontractors."

You say: "I had no control over their work."

They say: "You were still responsible."
Now your critical path delay is classified as Contractor-caused, thanks to a subcontractor you were forbidden from replacing.

HOW TO FIX IT:

Reinforce risk separation:
"The Contractor shall not be liable for delay, defect, disruption, or non-performance caused by Employer-nominated subcontractors unless such parties are under the Contractor's contractual control and the Contractor has meaningful authority to coordinate, replace, or enforce performance."

Insert performance safeguard:
"Where the Contractor cannot reasonably manage, replace, or enforce performance by the nominated subcontractor, the Employer shall retain responsibility for delay, defect, or disruption caused by that nominated subcontractor."

Link liability to access:
"Responsibility applies only where the Contractor has direct contractual authority, payment control, and programme influence."

Because if you do not control the actor,
you should not inherit the consequences of their actions.

WTF SCORING SYSTEM™

Metric	Score
WTF Factor	9.5/10 – Risk by Proxy
Risk Profile	CRITICAL – Transfer of liability without control
Verdict	REMOVE OR QUALIFY or SHIFT RISK back to nominating party

ENGINEERING TAKEAWAY:

If you did not choose them, cannot direct them, and cannot replace them,

Then you should not be the one writing the cheque when they fail.

"Fast, good, cheap—pick two." – Engineering Proverb

CLAUSE #49

"The Employer May, At Its Discretion, Require Acceleration without Any Entitlement to Additional Cost."

aka: *The Clause That Treats Acceleration Like a Charity Project*

ENGINEER'S TRANSLATION:

"Speed up the work. We will not pay you. But we will penalise you if you fail."

SATIRICAL INTERPRETATION:

This clause demands acceleration as if it were a favour, to be offered freely, not invoiced professionally.

It says:
"You will add shifts, compress your programme, re-sequence your work, and pay for the privilege."

You are expected to:

- Mobilise overtime labour.
- Expedite materials.
- Compress critical path.
- Burn through contingencies ...at your own cost.

This clause sees urgency as your problem, but not their budget item.

WHY THIS IS A PROBLEM:

This clause treats acceleration as a gift; it allows the Employer to demand faster work at no additional cost, converting urgency into free effort and progress into unpaid pressure. This clause demands urgent performance at the Contractor's cost, even when the need for acceleration arises from Employer delay, converting urgency into unpaid overtime.

Found in:

- Acceleration clauses in EPC and FIDIC-based government contracts
- "Discretionary programme adjustment" provisions
- Crisis-response sections in oil, gas, and power projects
- Middle East and defence-linked infrastructure projects

Its purpose?

- Enable the Employer to demand faster delivery.
- While denying the Contractor any pricing leverage
- Often used to recover Employer delays, disguised as Contractor initiative

LEGAL INSIGHT:

Acceleration is not free simply because the Employer needs the project recovered. If the Contractor is instructed to add labour, extend working hours, resequence works, expedite materials, or compress the programme, the contract should state whether that acceleration is voluntary, instructed, compensable, or part of the Contractor's existing obligation.

In *Walter Lilly & Co Ltd v Mackay*[62] [2012] EWHC 1773 (TCC), the court dealt extensively with delay, extensions of time, loss and expense, and proof of causation under a construction contract. The useful lesson here is evidential: if acceleration cost is to be recovered, the Contractor must preserve entitlement, record the instruction, prove the additional measures, and connect the cost to the instructed recovery effort. A clause that demands acceleration but denies cost relief turns programme recovery into unpaid crisis management.

WHERE THIS BREAKS THE BACK OF YOUR TEAM

The Employer's own delays push the project 6 weeks behind. They issue a letter:
"Clause 8.6 invoked. Acceleration required to restore baseline. Submit updated recovery plan. No additional cost will be entertained."

You raise a query.
No response.
You accelerate, under pressure.

At final account, your acceleration cost is rejected:
"Acceleration was discretionary. Clause 8.6: No entitlement."

You worked harder.
You delivered faster.
You earned nothing, except burnt labour and resentment.

HOW TO FIX IT:

Clarify voluntary vs. instructed:
"No acceleration shall be instructed unless jointly agreed and commercially valued."

62 Walter Lilly & Co Ltd v Mackay [2012] EWHC 1773 (TCC), United Kingdom (Technology and Construction Court).

Preserve claim rights:
"Where the Contractor accelerates in response to Employer delay, entitlement to cost and time adjustment shall remain intact."

Require written agreement:
"Instructed acceleration shall be subject to a written instruction, agreed valuation where practicable, and contemporaneous records of additional labour, plant, supervision, disruption, and expediting cost."

Because no one should be required to sprint, on someone else's mistake, and someone else's dime.

WTF SCORING SYSTEM™

Metric	Score
WTF Factor	9.6/10 – Rush Order Without the Order
Risk Profile	CRITICAL – Allows cost-free acceleration demand
Verdict	REQUIRE VARIATION APPROVAL or STRIKE entirely unless jointly agreed

ENGINEERING TAKEAWAY:

When acceleration is demanded without compensation, you are no longer a Contractor.

You are a volunteer on someone else's schedule.

"Experience is what you get when you didn't get what you wanted." – Randy Pausch

CLAUSE #50

"The Contractor Warrants that it is an Experienced Contractor and Has Independently Reviewed, Assessed, and Satisfied Itself as to the Completeness and Accuracy of the Contract Documents, and Shall not Rely Upon Any Explanations or Interpretations Provided By the Employer."

aka: *The Clause That Weaponizes Your Experience Against You*

ENGINEER'S TRANSLATION:

"You are an expert. Therefore, if anything goes wrong, you should have known better. And no, we will not explain ourselves."

SATIRICAL INTERPRETATION:

This clause flatters you. Then uses that flattery as a legal weapon.

It says:
"You are experienced, right? Then why did you rely on our verbal clarification? Why did you misread the spec? Why didn't you foresee the contradiction we buried on page 97?"

It is the contractual equivalent of:
"You're smart, so this must be your fault."

WHY THIS IS A PROBLEM:

This clause weaponizes your expertise; it flatters the Contractor's competence only to use it as a shield against all clarifications, all reliance, and all future claims. It flatters the Contractor's expertise to disqualify their rights, blocking claims, denying reliance on clarification, and shifting the burden for Employer-issued errors.

You will find this clause in:

- Recitals and Representations
- Tender declarations and acknowledgements
- Early clauses buried before the main Conditions begin.
- Contracts where Employers want to reverse contra proferentem without saying so.

Its impact:

- Denies reliance on Q&A clarifications.
- Nullifies ambiguity-based claims.
- Turns your "expertise" into a pre-allocated blame mechanism.

LEGAL INSIGHT:

Experience does not make a Contractor clairvoyant. It may justify holding a Contractor to clear contractual obligations, but it should not be used to erase Employer ambiguity, contradictory documents, missing information, or formal clarifications issued during tender.

In *Persimmon Homes Ltd v Ove Arup & Partners Ltd*[63] [2017] EWCA Civ 373, the Court of Appeal gave effect to clear risk-allocation wording in a negotiated commercial contract involving sophisticated parties. Applied here, the warning is simple: if the contract clearly says that the Contractor has reviewed, accepted, and cannot rely on explanations, that wording may be enforced. The answer is not to rely on expertise as a defence. The answer is to preserve reliance on written clarifications, Employer-issued information, and identified assumptions before signing.

WHERE THIS NULLIFIES YOUR RIGHT TO CLARITY

You relied on the BOQ that mismatched the drawing.
You raised a query.
No reply.
You proceeded based on logic and contract priority rules.
At final account, they reject your claim:
"Clause 1.3: You warranted that you are an experienced contractor and shall not rely on any explanation or interpretation from us."
Your logic? Irrelevant.
Your RFI (Request for Information)? Unacknowledged.
Your expertise? Now legally binding against you.

63 Persimmon Homes Ltd v Ove Arup & Partners Ltd [2017] EWCA Civ 373, United Kingdom (Court of Appeal).

HOW TO FIX IT:

Limit the clause:
"Contractor's experience shall not override Employer's duty to issue clear, coordinated, and complete documentation."

Add carve-outs:
"This warranty shall not preclude the Contractor from relying on written Employer clarifications, tender responses, issued drawings, assumptions expressly stated in the Contractor's offer, or instructions issued before execution."

Reject blind liability:
"No such clause shall be interpreted as acceptance of latent ambiguities, Employer-side discrepancies, or information gaps not reasonably identifiable before execution."

Because experience does not equal clairvoyance.
And a compliment should not become a conviction.

WTF SCORING SYSTEM™

Metric	Score
WTF Factor	9.7/10 – Compliment That Converts to Liability
Risk Profile	CRITICAL – Disqualifies claims through self-incrimination
Verdict	REMOVE OR REPHRASE or BALANCE with duty to issue clear scope

ENGINEERING TAKEAWAY:

If the contract praises your experience, check if it is also setting you up for absolute blame. Because in this clause, the smarter you are…

The easier it is to say, "You should have known."

Construction Lessons Series 018

"Delay analysis is history written by whoever owns the Primavera licence."

Tailpiece: The Clause That Was not in the Contract

This book may have made you smile.
At least a chuckle...?
It may have made you grimace.
It may even have made you reach for that one contract you have been meaning to read, properly.
But this is not just a satirical collection.

These clauses are real.
These stories are real.
And the consequences? Far from funny.

Some of these clauses have resulted in:

- Claims lost before they were filed.
- Contractors bankrupted on paper they never saw coming.
- Engineers blamed for logic they never approved.
- Thousands of workers demobilised because a drawing was "deemed" sufficient.
- And Project Managers walking offsite because their programme was no longer theirs to defend.

If you are in the industry long enough, you will meet people who lost their livelihood because of clauses like these. They did not lose on facts. They lost on footnotes.

Not because they were lazy.
Not because they were wrong.

But because they trusted language that was never written to protect them.
And that is the real clause that was not in the contract:
Common sense.

This book is for them.

For the Contractor who never got paid. For the planning engineer whose delay was declared "Contractor's own risk."

For the site supervisor who was told, "We are a bit busy now and can't approve that VO, but please proceed anyway."

We do not write about these clauses to make fun of contracts.
We write about them to take the power back.

Because if a clause feels unfair, unclear, or unnecessary,
It probably is.

And if it feels clever, it is probably dangerous!

But if you do not catch it early, it will catch you later.

Your next contract will not be perfect.
But with a red pen, a sharp question, and maybe a little sarcasm,
You just might survive it.

With sharp clauses, sharper instincts, and all due respect, wishing you fewer risks, stronger contracts, and absolutely no "deemed" anything.

– Jinoy Viswan

Epilogue: Same Clause, Different Law

Before we close, let me leave you with one more clause.

You will not find it in the Conditions of Contract.
It is not buried in the appendix.
And no, it does not come with a clause number.

But it decides more outcomes than any clause ever written.

It is called: **Applicable Law**.

A Project Manager once told me, with full confidence, that he had faced a similar dispute in India, won his claim, and now expected the same outcome on a UAE project.

"Same facts. Same issue. Same result, right?"

He had logic on his side.
He had fairness on his side.
He even had precedent; just not from the right country.

I told him, gently:

"What wins you a case in Mumbai may lose it in Muscat.
What is accepted in London may be inadmissible in Riyadh.
The clause did not change.
The system did."

That is the uncomfortable truth.

The same clause can be interpreted in diverse ways under different legal systems:

In Common Law, it may be subject to precedent and judicial reasoning.

In Civil Law systems, contractual outcomes may be driven primarily by codified provisions, sometimes with limited scope for judicial re-balancing unless good faith, abuse of rights, or mandatory statutory protections are engaged.

In Sharia-influenced jurisdictions, contractual principles may be overridden by moral equity.

And in Arbitration, outcomes will depend less on doctrine alone and more on how clearly the governing law, contractual intent, and commercial consequences are presented to the tribunal.

This is why contract strategy is not just about what you write.
It is about where it will be read.
And who will be reading it.

So the next time you see a clause and feel confident, pause.

Ask:

1. What law governs this contract?
2. How do that jurisdiction's courts or tribunals interpret this clause?
3. And is my confidence based on experience, or just familiarity with a different system?

Because in contract disputes, familiarity is not protection.
Only understanding is.

The same clause may represent fairness in one court… and finality in another.
It may invite flexibility in one system… and trigger strict liability in another.

So treat each clause with curiosity.
Each risk with humility.
And each jurisdiction with respect.

And if ever in doubt, remember:
Even the smartest contract becomes meaningless,
If you forget where its meaning will be decided.

– Jinoy Viswan

End Notes

1. Engineer- The person or entity appointed by the Employer to act on its behalf in administering the Contract. See Party Definitions.
2. *Chartbrook Ltd v Persimmon Homes Ltd* [2009] UKHL 38, United Kingdom (House of Lords).
3. *Investors Compensation Scheme Ltd v West Bromwich Building Society* [1998] 1 WLR 896, United Kingdom (House of Lords).
4. *Baird Textile Holdings Ltd v Marks & Spencer plc* [2001] EWCA Civ 274, United Kingdom (Court of Appeal).
5. *RTS Flexible Systems Ltd v Molkerei Alois Müller GmbH* [2010] UKSC 14, United Kingdom (Supreme Court).
6. *RTI Ltd v MUR Shipping BV* [2024] UKSC 18, United Kingdom (Supreme Court).
7. *Jet2.com Ltd v Blackpool Airport Ltd* [2012] EWCA Civ 417, United Kingdom (Court of Appeal).
8. *United Scientific Holdings Ltd v Burnley Borough Council* [1978] AC 904, United Kingdom (House of Lords).
9. *Behzadi v Shaftesbury Hotels Ltd* [1992] Ch 1, United Kingdom (Court of Appeal).
10. *Rock Advertising Ltd v MWB Business Exchange Centres Ltd* [2018] UKSC 24.
11. *RTS Flexible Systems Ltd v Molkerei Alois Müller GmbH* [2010] UKSC 14.
12. *Investors Compensation Scheme Ltd v West Bromwich Building Society* [1998] 1 WLR 896, United Kingdom (House of Lords).
13. *Chartbrook Ltd v Persimmon Homes Ltd* [2009] UKHL 38, United Kingdom (House of Lords).
14. *Abbey Developments Ltd v PP Brickwork Ltd* [2003] EWHC 1987 (TCC), United Kingdom (Technology and Construction Court).
15. *Compass Group UK and Ireland Ltd v Mid Essex Hospital Services NHS Trust* [2013] EWCA Civ 200, United Kingdom (Court of Appeal).
16. *National Carriers Ltd v Panalpina (Northern) Ltd* [1981] AC 675, United Kingdom (House of Lords).
17. *Macdonald Estates plc v Regenesis (2005) Dunfermline Ltd* [2007] CSOH 123, Scotland (Outer House, Court of Session).
18. *Australian Broadcasting Corporation v XIVth Commonwealth Games Ltd* (1988) 18 NSWLR 540, Australia (New South Wales Court of Appeal).

19. *Mid Essex Hospital Services NHS Trust v Compass Group UK and Ireland Ltd* [2013] EWCA Civ 200, United Kingdom (Court of Appeal).
20. *Gan Insurance Co Ltd v Tai Ping Insurance Co Ltd* [2001] EWCA Civ 1047, United Kingdom (Court of Appeal).
21. *Porton Capital Technology Funds v 3M UK Holdings Ltd* [2011] EWHC 2895 (Comm), United Kingdom (Commercial Court).
22. *Tele2 International Card Company SA v Post Office Ltd* [2009] EWCA Civ 9, United Kingdom (Court of Appeal).
23. *Photo Production Ltd v Securicor Transport Ltd* [1980] AC 827, United Kingdom (House of Lords).
24. *Heyman v Darwins Ltd* [1942] AC 356, United Kingdom (House of Lords).
25. *North Midland Building Ltd v Cyden Homes Ltd* [2018] EWCA Civ 1744, United Kingdom (Court of Appeal).
26. *Gaymark Investments Pty Ltd v Walter Construction Group Ltd* [1999] NTSC 143, Australia (Supreme Court of the Northern Territory).
27. *Tharsis Sulphur & Copper Co v McElroy & Sons* (1878) 3 App Cas 1040, United Kingdom (House of Lords).
28. *Multiplex Construction (UK) Ltd v Honeywell Control Systems Ltd* [2007] EWHC 447 (TCC), United Kingdom (Technology and Construction Court).
29. *Gaymark Investments Pty Ltd v Walter Construction Group Ltd* [1999] NTSC 143, Australia (Supreme Court of the Northern Territory).
30. *Multiplex Construction (UK) Ltd v Honeywell Control Systems Ltd* [2007] EWHC 447 (TCC), United Kingdom (Technology and Construction Court).
31. *Henry Boot Construction Ltd v Alstom Combined Cycles Ltd* [2005] EWCA Civ 814, United Kingdom (Court of Appeal).
32. *Socimer International Bank Ltd v Standard Bank London Ltd* [2008] EWCA Civ 116, United Kingdom (Court of Appeal).
33. *Khan v Miah* [2000] 1 WLR 2123, United Kingdom (House of Lords).
34. *MT Højgaard A/S v E.ON Climate & Renewables UK* [2017] UKSC 59, United Kingdom (Supreme Court).
35. *Mouchel Ltd v Van Oord UK Ltd* [2011] EWHC 72 (TCC), United Kingdom (Technology and Construction Court).
36. *Linden Gardens Trust Ltd v Lenesta Sludge Disposals Ltd* [1994] 1 AC 85, United Kingdom (House of Lords).
37. *MT Højgaard A/S v E.ON Climate & Renewables UK* [2017] UKSC 59, United Kingdom (Supreme Court).
38. *London Borough of Merton v Lowe (Builders) Ltd* (1981) 18 BLR 130, United Kingdom (Court of Appeal).
39. *Bremer Handelsgesellschaft mbH v Vanden Avenne Izegem PVBA* [1978] 2 Lloyd's Rep 109, United Kingdom (House of Lords).

40. *Bunge Corp v Tradax Export SA* [1981] 1 WLR 711, United Kingdom (House of Lords).
41. *Mitsui Construction Co Ltd v Attorney General of Hong Kong* [1986] 33 BLR 1, Hong Kong (Privy Council).
42. *Inntrepreneur Pub Co v East Crown Ltd* [2000] 2 Lloyd's Rep 611, United Kingdom (High Court).
43. *AXA Sun Life Services plc v Campbell Martin Ltd* [2011] EWCA Civ 133, United Kingdom (Court of Appeal).
44. *Abbey Developments Ltd v PP Brickwork Ltd* [2003] EWHC 1987 (TCC), United Kingdom (Technology and Construction Court).
45. *Costain Ltd v Bechtel Ltd* [2005] EWHC 1018 (TCC), United Kingdom (Technology and Construction Court).
46. *Shell UK Ltd v Total UK Ltd* [2010] EWCA Civ 180, United Kingdom (Court of Appeal).
47. *Transocean Drilling UK Ltd v Providence Resources plc* [2016] EWCA Civ 372, United Kingdom (Court of Appeal).
48. *Education 4 Ayrshire Ltd v South Ayrshire Council* [2009] CSOH 146, Scotland (Outer House, Court of Session).
49. *MT Højgaard A/S v E.ON Climate & Renewables UK* [2017] UKSC 59, United Kingdom (Supreme Court).
50. *Multiplex Construction (UK) Ltd v Honeywell Control Systems Ltd* [2007] EWHC 447 (TCC), United Kingdom (Technology and Construction Court).
51. *Balfour Beatty Building Ltd v Chestermount Properties Ltd* (1993) 62 BLR 1, United Kingdom (Commercial Court).
52. *Molloy v Liebe* (1910) 102 LT 616, Privy Council.
53. *Tharsis Sulphur & Copper Co v McElroy & Sons* (1878) 3 App Cas 1040, United Kingdom (House of Lords).
54. *MT Højgaard A/S v E.ON Climate & Renewables UK Ltd* [2017] UKSC 59, United Kingdom (Supreme Court).
55. *Linden Gardens Trust Ltd v Lenesta Sludge Disposals Ltd* [1994] 1 AC 85, United Kingdom (House of Lords).
56. *MT Højgaard A/S v E.ON Climate & Renewables UK* [2017] UKSC 59, United Kingdom (Supreme Court).
57. *Plant Construction plc v Clive Adams Associates* [2000] EWHC Technology 119, United Kingdom (Technology and Construction Court).
58. *RSP Architects Planners & Engineers v Mott MacDonald Singapore Pte Ltd* [2014] SGHC 72, Singapore (High Court).
59. *Canada Steamship Lines Ltd v The King* [1952] AC 192, United Kingdom (Privy Council).
60. *Persimmon Homes Ltd v Ove Arup & Partners Ltd* [2017] EWCA Civ 373, United Kingdom (Court of Appeal).

61. *Percy Bilton Ltd v Greater London Council* [1982] 1 WLR 794, United Kingdom (House of Lords).
62. *Walter Lilly & Co Ltd v Mackay* [2012] EWHC 1773 (TCC), United Kingdom (Technology and Construction Court).
63. *Persimmon Homes Ltd v Ove Arup & Partners Ltd* [2017] EWCA Civ 373, United Kingdom (Court of Appeal).

The WTF Clausebook – Volume 1

"To the extent not otherwise inconsistent with the foregoing..."

If you have ever read a clause like that, and still had no idea what it meant, this book is for you.

The WTF Clausebook: Volume 1 is a satirical survival guide for engineers, project managers, contract managers, and battle-worn contractors. It dives headfirst into fifty of the most baffling, one-sided, and dangerously vague clauses found in real-world construction contracts.

Each clause is dissected with equal parts:

- Legal insight
- Dark humour
- Real-world case law (yes, the kind that ends in court, or liquidation)

From "reasonable endeavours" that do nothing of the sort, to time bars that punish you for being 48 hours late while the Employer is 6 months behind, this book unpacks the fine print that breaks spirits, budgets, and occasionally, companies.

Inside this volume:

- Fifty weaponised clauses straight from the field
- Footnotes and legal references for the doubters
- Case summaries that explain how it all went sideways
- The WTF Scoring System™, not legally binding, but emotionally accurate

JINOY VISWAN is not a lawyer. He is the person lawyers call when the contractor is actually right. With three decades of international EPC and contracts management experience, he has seen more fine print than a forensic printer technician. This book is part therapy, part warning, and fully grounded in lived experience.

Volume 2 is coming. The next fifty clauses are worse.

www.ingramcontent.com/pod-product-compliance
Lightning Source LLC
LaVergne TN
LVHW022154200926
848481LV00006B/1738